LOVE

YOU

LIKE

THE

SKY

LOVE
YOU
LIKE
THE
SKY

SURVIVING
THE SUICIDE
OF A BELOVED

SARAH NEUSTADTER, PhD

SPARKPRESS

Published by SparkPress, a BookSparks imprint,
A division of SparkPoint Studio, LLC
Tempe, Arizona, USA, 85281
www.gosparkpress.com

Published 2019
Printed in the United States of America
(pbk) ISBN: 978-1-943006-88-5
(ebk) ISBN: 978-1-943006-89-2
Library of Congress Control Number: 2019931368

Interior design by Tabitha Lahr

For all those with broken hearts

contents

despair

shifting

beauty

author's note

The writing of this book spans the course of nine years, from 2009 to 2018. I wrote large chunks in the first three years after my boyfriend, John died. Early on, an editor commented that with the gravity of this kind of tragedy, the book might be better if I had time to mature and sit with the experience, and then write about what I'd learned in hindsight. Her comment stuck with me, but I still pursued my writing during those early years. It was imperative that I release my raw, unpolished emotion and memories onto the page, with or without aged wisdom. Eventually, however, I stepped away from the manuscript. I needed a "vacation" from the heaviness of suicide and grief. I took such a long break, in fact, that I gave up on writing and wanting to share this book. I was more interested in living in the "light," as is often the case in Los Angeles, and experiencing the fun I'd missed during my years of darkness.

It wasn't until recently, in seeing how many people—especially public figures—are committing suicide and overdosing, and recognizing the unbearable despair these deaths are inevitably leaving in their wake, that I felt a beckoning to complete this book. The world has become a much harder place to live these past few years, and many are seeking an exit, a return to a more innocent state. This book is for a new generation of survivors; I hope it will help them navigate trauma and suffering from a more spiritual, self-aware perspective.

As the ten-year anniversary of John's suicide approaches, I recognize that this story is no longer my own but the collective's. It's about how far we've come from our original innocence and how, through our heartbreak and loss, we can find our way back home without having to literally, kill ourselves.

introduction

When I was twenty-nine and a third-year doctoral student in psychology, my beloved boyfriend of two and a half years—the man I intended to spend the rest of my life with and my fellow psychology student—took his life by throwing himself beside the train tracks in our small town of Mountain View in Northern California. John had turned thirty-six days prior.

In the wake of his death, I sank so far into darkness that I could barely muster the will to get through another day. I wanted to die. The pain of missing him was unbearable. The thought of living the rest of my life, years upon years, without him filled me with hopelessness and despair. I didn't want to do it. I couldn't do it. Yet I had no choice. I could never kill myself and inflict the same kind of pain and suffering I was now feeling on my own loved ones. I was trapped. I knew, though, that if I was going to be alive, I had to try to make the most of it, find some reason for my loss and why I was going through what I was going through. I knew I needed to heal, but I didn't know how. I felt alone and alienated from my friends, family, and peers. They'd never experienced this kind of loss—the death of a partner. Nor had they experienced a death so tragic and shocking before.

In the first year after John died, very little helped ease my pain. Nothing anyone who hadn't experienced this kind of death did or said could help me. I needed guidance from others who had gone through it. I needed to know how others who had been in a similar situation were carrying on with the rest of their lives without their beloved. How had they made peace with their own mortality and the choice made by their partner? How had they kept on living with their hearts damaged as they were?

I searched in vain for books about other women in existential agony over the death of their husbands or beloveds. I found how-to guides for suicide grief and a couple of memoirs about becoming a widow but no memoirs about surviving the suicide of a partner or books that voiced the longing I felt to join John in death. None of the books I found mirrored the depth of my pain or offered me a concrete roadmap for navigating this kind of existential hell. None of the books provided believable assurance that my life would ever feel better without John.

From within my despair, I found no relief in how-to manuals and other self-help books. They did not empathize with my loss. I felt talked to and coached at, not joined with. The authors' words of hope felt dismissive and minimizing of my pain. As a spiritually oriented person, I also found that these books did not provide relevant answers on how to help me carry my heartache through all the hours, days, weeks, and years ahead of me. I wanted to read a book that voiced the desperate, soulful longing of a being separated from a soul mate by death. I wanted to learn how to reconnect with John in spirit.

Eight months after John died, I started writing emails to him. In them, I told him the story of us, his death, and my grief. I sent each email to his former Yahoo address, knowing I wouldn't get a response but needing to send them nevertheless. This book is a compilation of those emails, plus some blog posts, written from within the eye of the storm of grief and not from an outside perspective looking in.

I've organized these writings into three categories that reflect the organic unfolding of my healing process within the first three years following John's suicide: despair, shifting, and beauty. (Because of this organizational decision, the emails are not all in chronological order.) At the end of each section, I provide more professionally based psychological guidance on how to navigate the grief I've been exploring. I call these "The Maps."

At the back of the book is a section on transformational practices, as well as a list of resources I found helpful for self-healing and reestablishing a life after John's suicide. The resources have a spiritual bent to them. Pick and choose what resonates for you.

This book is meant to serve as a companion in grief for any survivor left behind without his or her beloved. It's also meant to help anyone suffering from deep depression or suicidal longings. My hope is that in reading about my journey of wrestling with John's suicide—and my own mortality—you will find a way to make sense of your own loss.

May my loss and self-healing process encourage and facilitate your own healing. Please know that even though you feel alone, you are not alone in this. Others are going through this darkness right now, and others have gone through it before you. I have been in your exact location of hell, and I have gotten out. Just know, perhaps in some vague distant way, that you will too.

despair

Despair is about the intensity of my grief, and this section may be too heavy for some readers. It may, however, sit just right for others who can relate to a sudden, tragic loss and possibly their own feelings of suicidal ideation.

This emotional rawness is a reality of the pain that most people in the throes of this kind of grief, or the friends and family of those grieving, often gloss over, minimize, or avoid because of how disturbing and uncomfortable it can be for other people. In our culture, we don't quite have any socially accepted, healthy, normalized rituals and grace periods for authentic mourning. Therefore, collectively, we don't know how to support each other through grief and raw emotion. *Despair* emphasizes and acknowledges the pain and existential agony of losing a loved one to suicide and, hopefully, gives you, the reader, permission to feel these feelings and have your experience. These feelings are a natural product of the grief, shock, and trauma we experience when a loved one dies. And they facilitate the healing process.

When we avoid despair, we shortchange our mourning process and minimize what has been lost. Speeding through despair and not giving it its due diligence can cause unresolved grief later in life. So the invitation here is to take some time and connect deeply to your feelings, no matter how painful they are.

....

Dear John,

I want to tell you the story of us, from my perspective, before it fades into the memories of all the years to come. Given that you're in spirit form, you already know my version of the story—every nuance of emotion and every thought that's ever washed through me. But I want to write it down. I need to put it into words and send it to you. I can't let myself forget a single moment. I have to document it all. I know not to expect a reply from you. I've no hope for that. Yet still I write.

Hard to begin. I started writing two weeks ago—thought I could mimic something akin to Joan Didion's *The Year of Magical Thinking*. Not quite. As I sat in the Rose Reading Room at the 42nd Street library, the process of reliving that day at the hospital had tears streaming down my face as I continually blew my nose with thin crispy toilet tissue. When I left the library, I immediately bought a pack of cigarettes and smoked. It was raining, but not hard enough to require an umbrella. I felt broken again, drained, like a pile of wet laundry. The cigarette was a weak comfort for all I've lost, and all I'd just dragged myself through emotionally. I know you wouldn't like me smoking. Remember when we were at a party at Dan's house and I had a couple of puffs of his herbal cigarette? You thought it was a real one and looked at me like I was a leper. Your condemning look, however, with your wide eyes and upper lip curling into that boyish smile, still looked sweet and loving. You were surprised more so than judgmental. And it was darling, as usual.

I don't even know if your email address still works. I guess I'll find out when I send this out into the void of cyberspace.

I love you always,
Love,
Sarah

John,

Yes. Your email account still works. The first email didn't bounce back. I'll continue to write to you, if only for myself.

I'm on the plane heading back to California. Been a vitalizing trip home, and I'm sad to leave, yet couldn't possibly continue pumping myself through the city. Manhattan's my hometown, but it's intense. I'll miss the energy, the creativity, the humor, and my dear friends and family. I was sitting at JFK, waiting to board, and that old, familiar, melancholy ache began . . . the missing of you. Why do airports stir up such grief? I search for you. I imagine your light blue jeans, catch a glimpse of your striped polo shirt as you round the corner, see the edge of your sneaker, your blond curls . . . and then there you are. Walking towards me. I search you out and search and search . . . and my eyeballs strain. Like if I stare long enough I can materialize you from thin air. I only have this false hope at airports. You don't appear. Disappointment. Again. I turn my head from the crowd and resent my life for not being a stupid Hollywood film where these things could maybe just happen.

The ache moves up into my throat and waits impatiently to come out through tears. I can feel it building. Something's building, waiting for release.

Traveling with you was always warm and delicious—encapsulated in our own bubble, floating through arbitrary space. Like the time we sat on the floor in a corner at the noisy Vegas airport and read Eckhart Tolle together, our bodies folded into each other like liquid. Or when we passed through security in Amarillo . . . I put my sneakers back on and noticed the tiles sparkling. I stood up, looked at you standing behind me, and felt completely at home. The terminal was cold and air-conditioned. You were warm as you lay your head in my lap and sprawled out on the empty row of seats and napped. We'd almost always miss our flights because we'd get so comfortable and absorbed in our own world. We often forgot the very reason we happened to be at the airport.

I cried through takeoff and floated back in my seat, eyes closed, surrendering to the pressure. Only once we were in the air did I open my eyes.

I'm seated between four couples, each one cuter than the next. I'm alone in the aisle seat and watch them from the corner of my eye. The couple on my immediate left is from Spain and they're watching the in-house movie, some Julia Roberts flick. The couple to my right is working quietly on a crossword puzzle while she nurses a glass of wine and he sips an Amstel Light. The woman in the row in front is wearing a winter hat and curled up in her husband's lap. I feel orphaned in my aisle seat. The other night at a bar on the Upper West Side comes back to me.

"Do you have a boyfriend?" Israeli Girl Number 1 asked.

"Are the boys in California cute?" Israeli Girl Number 2 asked.

"No, I don't have a boyfriend. And, um, yeah, the boys in California are cute."

"How old are you?" they both inquired.

"Thirty," I said. They gave me a strange look, and stopped asking questions about boys.

I'm devoted to you still, even though others in my life won't be happy to hear this. They want me to get on with things, be angry at you, blame you, let you go. I can't do that. I try and pretend I'm moving on, letting go of you by not talking about you so much and by engaging in social activities so the outside world doesn't see the constant burn in my heart, my ever-present connection and dedication to you, even now. But nobody understands.

I miss you, baby. I'm in your space, meeting you halfway in the sky.

Where are you?

Sarah

....

John,

I woke up this morning and stayed in that in-between state—not quite awake and not quite asleep. It was there that I saw you. You were fuzzy and your outline blurred and shifted like you were out of focus. I wish I could've held on to your image longer but you slipped through my consciousness and were gone in seconds. I live for those dreams, for those moments where I can see you. They get me through the days.

Have you ever wondered about the countless twists and turns of our lives that brought you and me to the same place at the same time? I think about that often.

Our graduate class consisted of twenty-eight aspiring psychologists, divided into two cohorts. On the first day of orientation, we all sat in a circle and in typical California spiritual-psychology-school-fashion, went around and shared about ourselves. I scoped out the room for cute guys but didn't really see any, so that was sort of a disappointment. You weren't there yet. As I came to find out later, you always ran late since you juggled three jobs.

During the snack break in the courtyard, I hovered around the cheese plate, talking to Mary and Ashley about housing. I looked up briefly and saw you across the way. You looked sunny. Your dirty blond, shoulder-length curls, warm smile, and that astonishingly bright orange T-shirt . . . even your goatee made you seem boyish, like a hippie and a jock all rolled into one. You looked my way. I avoided eye contact and pushed a lock of auburn hair off my face. I know you saw me. I remember thinking you were cute and feeling grateful for at least one cute guy in the program, but then talking myself out of it by saying you really weren't that cute and besides, nothing would ever happen. The New Yorker in me was also secretly critical of that fact that you were late to our orientation. I mean, we were embarking on our PhDs . . . what could be more important than showing up on time for that? I'd had so many heartaches in New York with men who were often late (foreign men who operated on foreign time). So, without my consciously being aware of it, you immediately lost a point in my book. I also secretly resented that I hadn't gotten to hear your introductory spiel about how you came to our school but had to sit through everyone else's.

The next day was our two-day cohort orientation retreat in the Santa Cruz Mountains. We sat on pillows and BackJacks in a light-filled, octagonal room in the middle of a redwood forest. Our first icebreaker was to take an hour and collage or draw our "spiritual autobiographies"—which was an eye-opening way of considering my life story. When we were done, we presented them to the group. Yikes. The room was filled with silent excitement as we got lost in our own worlds and contemplated the major ups and downs, the pivotal life events, and the transformative people who had influenced our journeys and informed our sense of self in relationship to something greater. How had we stumbled and fallen or assertively marched toward the place we were in? It was definitely quite the revealing icebreaker. After we each shared our work, we felt bonded, like we'd found a long lost family. I had wandered through my life feeling like a spiritual outsider, and now I had finally found a place where I felt seen and understood.

You and I didn't talk much that weekend. Maybe some chitchat once at lunch, I don't really remember. Your autobiographical presentation showed your many experiences with fundamentalist Christianity: bonfires of the spirit at Jesus Camp (I hadn't known that was actually a thing) and your education at Oral Roberts University in Oklahoma (apparently a well-known fundamentalist Christian institution I'd never heard of in New York). I couldn't relate to you as yet and convinced myself you were strange and definitely not for me. But I do remember taking a walk through the woods and seeing you sitting by yourself on a hidden ledge overlooking a stream. You looked beached. I admired your ability to be quiet and alone while everyone else seemed compelled to socialize and do things together as a way of alleviating the anxiety and newness of the situation. This was attractive. I quietly walked on by and let you be.

We sat in class together, six hours a day, and your cuteness called to me despite my efforts to avoid it. I stared at your back as you sat in a straight, easy posture. You had the strong, lean build of someone used to working out. I could tell that underneath your collection of striped polo shirts your body was chiseled, sexy. Oh no. This wasn't good. I couldn't let myself be attracted to you or think of you as real dating material. I was looking for my life partner. I didn't necessarily care about getting married, per se, but I wanted to find my "teammate," ya know? I was serious and ready. You were in my cohort at grad school for god's sake (too incestuous), and with your defined jaw, perfect lips, slightly tanned skin, and huge, cerulean-blue eyes you were so classically gorgeous you had to be a player. At twenty-seven I was too old to play games or get played. I did my best to ignore your cuteness.

But I have a thing for men's hands. I always check them out. And yours caught my attention right away. They were simply the most beautiful, sculpted, strong hands I've ever seen. The hands of Michelangelo's David. I couldn't help but discreetly stare (all day) at the intricate sculpture of your languid wrists, large, rugged palms, and tapered fingers as you held your hands together with care or slowly lowered your middle and ring finger into your palm as you spoke. Your hands I couldn't deny.

It wasn't until the night before Halloween at our school talent show that I became fully aware of my attraction to you. Our Harry Potter–like Hogwarts school of psychology was cheesy, with its talents shows, no-desk-or-shoe policies, and the guitars and teddy bear in the lounge. I twiddled my Japanese stone earrings and waited impatiently through sword-wielding belly dancers, magicians, and over-enunciating poetry slammers. I was really only secretly there to see you. Finally, at the last act, you came on stage wearing a shapeless dark green velvet dress a grandma might wear, with a Christmas stocking on your head and an oven mitt on your hand. We laughed at your grandma-drag, of course. And later you told me you wanted the audience to laugh *at* you to alleviate their anxiety about assessing if you were talented or not. You were always trying to lessen the burden of others. On stage next to you, one of your housemates, an older woman named Jean—in her fifties, with a short bowl haircut— played a honky-tonk saloon version of "Somewhere Over the Rainbow." Despite your efforts to distract and enter- tain us with your drag, our attention was immediately drawn to your voice, which made any judgment of your talent completely irrelevant. You sang in tune, fluid and clear. Your voice was a smooth baritone sailing straight from your core and filling up the room like you'd done this a thousand times. The song was clearly dear to your heart and your smile shined as you flirted with the audience in your dress. Wow. I had no idea you were so talented. It was like being among greatness. As if an undercover celebrity was coming out of hiding. Something in me melted. And just like everyone else in the room, I was smitten and couldn't take my eyes off you.

I lingered after the show, hoping to talk to you and compliment you. I wanted you to come to the bar with Sophie, Brandon, Ben, Lisa, and a few others. But you were busy giving out hugs, like you usually did. I hadn't noticed before how many people at school you seemed to know. You hugged faculty, administration, upperclassmen, and randoms I'd never seen. Apparently, I was the latecomer to the John fan club. I watched you from the corner of my eye as I chatted with our friends, hoping you'd be as magnetically compelled to come over to me as I was to you. But you weren't. Did you even notice me that night? So I took off, and as I pulled out of the school parking lot and turned my head, I saw you hold the door open for a woman and then hug her goodbye. A stab pierced my chest. I turned my gaze back to the dark road and headed to meet everyone but you.

Writing this pulls me closer to you and keeps you near. My act of devotion.

Your greatest admirer,
Sarah

....

Dear John,

I'm ridiculously shy when it comes to men I like. Did you know that about me? It doesn't come across that way and friends say I always appear confident. I don't know how I look on the outside, but I'm most definitely not confident when it comes to the guy I'm crushing on. I can barely make eye contact or string a coherent sentence together without stumbling. If something's gonna happen between me and a guy, I depend on my friends for wing support. I'm that shy. And this is weird, considering my past as a player in New York and the number of men I've been with.

The more I resisted you, the more my attraction grew. From Halloween on, my crush grew daily. In the mornings I'd blast my music and dance as I got dressed, feeling curiously energized and excited to go to school and see you. I was happy to simply be in class with you all day long and observe you. We tended to sit at opposite sides of the classroom, and since our classes were held in circles, we'd typically end up facing each other. I felt this line of energy between us, and the current was strong. If we happened to sit next to each other, the current grew even stronger, and I could barely keep my eyes off the side of your body. I tried balancing the number of times I looked at you with the number of times I looked around the room, just to play it cool. It helped a lot when you spoke up in class because it gave me free rein to look at your face.

You became everyone's favorite. How could we resist your white Mickey Mouse hoodie no grown man should ever wear and your big, innocent blue eyes, so light, like the sky? Or your warm hugs and that low, rumbling Texan-Midwestern drawl, or the day you showed up to class fifteen minutes late wearing mismatched sneakers? Sometimes in class, your eyes fixed on someone, you'd randomly get the giggles and let out this long, sweet, full-bodied laugh that ended with you wiping tears and saying, "Ooohh that's so good," and then giggling some more. Your movements in our (mandatory) Aikido class were graceful. You were so light on your feet, even us ladies could flip and drop you. Our sensei loved to use you for demonstrations, of course. Everything about you was light, bright, and sweet. People came up to you all day for your hugs. It became a thing. I was shy about going up to you directly for one, or going up to you in general for that matter, so I'd creep up with someone else, they'd get a hug from you, and then I'd piggyback after them and say something lame like, "Hey, I want a John hug too."

Your charms were grounds for me not to like you. If I didn't put a check on my feelings, I knew, I'd probably get hurt. (Fuck was I right.) So I made up a "cons" list about why I shouldn't like you:

1. With a body and looks like yours, you were definitely a player, and after my years in New York, I was tired of the games.
2. You probably had girls clamoring for your attention, like most pretty boys do, and therefore wouldn't lift a finger to get to know a woman.

3. You most certainly weren't into me.
4. You proselytized the teachings of your spiritual teacher, Byron Katie, way too much.
5. You came from a heavy Christian background; mine was orthodox Jewish. We would not be compatible, and fundamentalist Christianity was just too weird for me.
6. You had attended a fundamentalist Christian college in Oklahoma. Once again, weird.
7. You spent summers as a teenager at Jesus camp. Enough said.
8. You weren't intellectual (like my New York background). You were more of a spiritually abstract thinker. Some classmates thought you were Jesus-like. I didn't understand yet why they thought that.
9. I had a hard time following your thought process as you spoke.
10. I couldn't figure you out.
11. If I didn't end up with a Jewish man or a man who converted to Judaism, my parents would disown me (so they'd said).

You spoke of abstractions of consciousness as if from another dimension, trying to translate something that couldn't be put into words. You'd often start a sentence and then stop midway because a new thought would come through your mind. You'd glance off, as if questioning its mysterious arrival, and then follow its train of thought out loud. And you spoke slowly. Very slowly—too slowly for my fast-talking, New York, stream-of-consciousness mind—and you paused often to get clear on your thoughts. You frequently talked about yourself in the third person, as if you were separate from yourself and observing what you were doing and saying as it was happening. Your deep, rumbling voice was soothing, but I'd often get entranced and lost, unable to follow you as you began.

"I have the thought that, um . . . I notice fear—I watch for . . . sometimes in class when fear rises in me—this body-mind . . . [pause] . . . and gets expressed . . . the fear, um . . . my desire to step back, uh . . ." You paused and looked intently into the space in front of you, trying to hold on to your thoughts. "And uh . . . I wait to see . . . what the don't-know-mind has to . . . [pause] . . . when I trust someone else or more silence to give me . . . I have the thought that . . . there's confusion when I'm believing I . . . [pause] . . . when there's the belief that this me has something really important to say—and I notice I can continue doing what I've always done or not. Until I don't."

Your speech took getting used to, and it felt like you were talking in koans or riddles where both sides of the point were expressed and then negated. During our first year, I didn't know that the reason you spoke this way was because of your narcolepsy, because the medication you'd been on for over fifteen years, Provigil, a heavy stimulant to keep you awake, had this unfortunate, confusing, and mind-bending effect. About nine months later, when we were working on a paper together, I tried half a pill to see if it would help me focus. Within half an hour, my thoughts started to race. In order to speak I had to grab a thought by the horns as it ran by and hold it tightly, because if I didn't, the next thought appeared so quickly I'd drop the old thought and rush to pick up the new one. I couldn't get anything done. I also couldn't stop talking and gazing listlessly around the room. Only then did I gain any sense of what it must be like for you.

Your speech required me to be patient. During your long pauses, no matter what our conversation was about, I often lost track of what you were saying and drifted away into the vastness of your eyes. Their lightness was enchanting. But still, I used the fact that your speech was confusing as evidence for why I couldn't like you and why we'd never match. And besides, you were so not interested in me; you hardly talked to me.

Things changed on your birthday like some kind of magic. I know you remember. It was the point of no turning back, where I couldn't hide my feelings behind my lame excuses anymore. The night started at the creamery in Palo Alto. Because you loved breakfast, our classmates celebrated your birthday with a "breakfast dinner." Twenty of us sat squished around a long table. You ordered a chocolate and peanut butter milkshake — your favorite —and passed it around the table so we could each taste. Delicious. You and I exchanged a knowing look about how good it was. At the end of the dinner-breakfast you stood up and raised your empty milkshake glass. (Your speech somehow became clear and smooth in front of an audience; perhaps this had something to do with your acting background.)

"Friends, lovers, brothers, and sisters, I am beyond grateful for each and every one of you bringing your beautiful selves and allowing me to receive the gift of you on my birthday. Cheers to you delicious, yummy, yummy people." We laughed and toasted you. "But right quick . . ." You waved your hand. "Before we depart for the evening, please give me the gift of just one more thing. No one's leaving here without a hug from me."

You stood in the doorway, and a single-file line ran through the whole diner, as if we were waiting to sit on Santa's lap. Customers stared at us, puzzled. I was grinning from ear to ear, thoroughly amused.

"Only John could get away with this," Ben said, deadpan, twirling a dreadlock in his fingers. His turn was next.

"Come here brother," you said laughing, arms stretched open. Ben stepped forward. You swallowed him in a strong hug.

"Mm. So good to see you, bro. Thank you."

Ben's flat expression cracked into a smile. "Good to be here, John." He hugged back.

"Ahh," you sighed. "Come here, Yushiko. Let's have a Bramberry sandwich." You grabbed Ben's wife, Yushiko, who stood on the side with her arms crossed, and brought her into the hug.

"Mm. Yummy. You didn't think I'd let you leave without a hug, Yushiko, did you?"

Her mouth twitched then she let out a laugh. "Mr. John," she said.

"Happy birthday to me. Mm. Mm. It's so good. Thank you both for being you and for being here with me. Bro, I'm looking forward to picking up our conversation real soon."

Mary, who was next, jumped right into your arms and squeezed you tight like she was getting her John fix for the day. And on and on the line continued, until the restaurant floor had cleared and each of us had given you a piece of ourselves, and you were exuberant with your birthday gift. In exchange, we left with a share of your love. Classic you. And a memory we'll have for the rest of our lives. And with that, I was wonderstruck, smiling the whole way through. *Who is this guy? Like, how is he real?*

The festivities continued later that evening at a bar in Mountain View, the town you lived in. You didn't directly invite me and I felt shy about going, but I went anyways thanks to our friend Lisa's prodding. Dressed in ripped jeans and a black racer-back tank, I arrived while you were on your third Irish coffee. Coffee was your drink of choice that night because it helped with your narcolepsy and kept you awake. You didn't usually drink coffee, though, because it's not recommended for narcolepsy, but this was a special occasion.

You stood up, bowed, extended your hand to Lisa like a southern gentleman, and asked her to join you in the Texas two-step. Next it was Mary's turn, and then Ashley's. I watched as you held these women close, one hand around their waist and the other holding their hand. I wondered if you'd ask me to dance and felt nervous you wouldn't. But I overheard you saying that you were asking all the women for a dance as a birthday gift to yourself. My heart sped up. I was relieved but nervous. You got to me last.

I was intimidated by your sweetness, your charm, your grace. What could I possibly contribute to what was already so beautiful? What if I couldn't keep up with the steps? Partner dancing wasn't my forte and dancing with a man had always felt stressful—like wading in icy water and deliberating whether to go in. But even more daunting, I'd be dancing with you! Touching you. Could the skin and bones of my body hold the mush inside me and protect it from sloshing on the floor? I thought I might collapse in your arms.

I was distracting myself with a conversation with Jeff when you tapped me on the shoulder.

"Will you have this dance?"

You held both palms out. I took them and it began.

"One, two, two, one. One, two, two, one!" you murmured in my ear to the beat, guiding me along. I picked it up, and we flowed around the bar. Warmth rolled off your body. You smelled sweet and slightly sweaty, like Irish cream and Old Spice Ultra Sport. Our chemistry was undeniable. I listened to the purr of your voice and my body seemed to melt as we moved in sync to the music. Time disappeared. I got lost. I'd never felt this comfortable dancing with anyone. It was like our bodies were marked for dancing. Several songs later, I looked up and blinked. Where was I? Our friends were watching us quizzically.

"Where'd you learn to dance like this?" I asked.

"Saloons in Texas."

Well duh, of course. It was my first taste of your cowboy past. We continued to dance. You added steps, twirled me and held me against your chest—a world unto its own. I leaned into you and it felt like resting. I could have danced with you for hours and not noticed anything else in the world. But after some time, Lisa came up and broke the spell. You looked uncomfortable. I guess it was your birthday get-together, after all, and I shouldn't be hogging you. I excused myself to the restroom.

My heart was beating in my stomach as the adrenaline of our chemistry coursed through my body. I exhaled against the bathroom door. When I got back, you, Lisa, Ashley, and I danced together as a group. I was disappointed it wasn't the two of us anymore but got over it. There were moments, though, where the others drifted for a second and you and I came together in a movement. Those moments were like a question suspended in the air: would we continue dancing together, as we should, and ignore social etiquette? The question lingered. But as the others joined back in the dance, the answer, continually, was no.

And that was that. We danced until closing, then scuttled out the door. As I drove away slowly, I watched you walk home. I wouldn't call it walking though. You danced—your arms stretched out as if holding an invisible partner, two-stepping her blissfully into the night. A happy prince. I gazed at you in awe as you twirled your princess and two-stepped through the dark eucalyptus trees and out of sight. It was then I knew I had to be with you.

The next day you sent us this email:

Thanks for making my day yesterday. Those who were there in spirit were appreciated as well. Thanks for eating at a breakfast diner at dinnertime with me, for standing in line to let me take you in one by one, Barbara & Jean for opening your home and inviting the finest to fellowship and gab. Thanks to the ladies and gentlemen who "Texas two-stepped" the night away with me. I floated back to my bed after an extremely sweet trip between Castro Street and home. I was so engulfed with gratefulness for sharing the day with each of you and also appreciating the altered state of consciousness that the Irish coffees offered me. I woke up a newer man with some priceless memories to access whenever I want. Hugs all around,
John

Your gentleness washes over me and brings me to tears like you're here beside me. And in these moments I am in love.

Yours,
Sarah

....

Dear John,

We sat at the white marble bar of an Italian restaurant in Mountain View—the one where the bartender had a little crush on us. It was our third official date and we were fully absorbed in each other. That night you revealed to me that your dad regularly beat you, your brother, and your mom when you were three and four. I was shocked. Since I'd known you, you didn't seem to have the resentful air of a person struggling to overcome an abusive childhood. In fact, before you shared this with me you'd described your father as "the most amazing dad in the world." At school I had sometimes overheard you on the phone telling him he was the greatest father a boy could have and how "beyond grateful" you were for him in your life. "I love you, Dad," you said slowly at the end of each phone call. Your open appreciation of your dad was beautiful to hear. And because of your extraordinary appreciation for him, I never would have imagined how violent he had been.

Through your disjointed sentences I pieced together the fragments of your childhood, and you began to make more sense.

Your family used to live on a ranch in western Texas—where your dad worked. Each night he'd come home from drinking and beat your mom, often with a belt.

I could see you as a small, wide-eyed boy, running into her lap to protect her. You were thrown headfirst into a wall; your dad was on a warpath toward your mom. You hated seeing her get hurt and paid the price for it night after night. You felt ashamed you couldn't protect her. Finally, one night, your mom took you and your brother Luke and ran away to her parents' house in Kansas. John, I'm sorry you lived through that. I'm sorry for the damage the abuse caused you in so many ways and on so many levels throughout the course of your life. It affected your brain, your emotions, your sense of safety, the way you handle stress, the way you seemed perpetually on silent guard. More than you even knew. It all makes sense now.

What was most shocking was how easily and naturally you forgave your father and reached out to him when you were seven. You insisted on visiting him in Texas every summer. It still amazes me how different you and Luke were. He refused to talk to your dad and wanted nothing to do with him, until just recently actually. In the bar then, and forever afterwards, I was mesmerized by your extraordinary capacity for unconditional love. Your dad never forgave himself. And I wondered if you even thought there was anything to forgive. You said your dad had one of the biggest hearts you'd ever known and that when you visited, he was overjoyed to have you in his life. He showered you with hugs, showed you off to the whole town, and never ceased telling you (and everyone else) what a miracle you were in his life (this part I heard from him, when we visited Texas after we'd been together four months—I have to distinguish, 'cause you would never talk of yourself so immodestly).

With my elbow on the bar, chin in hand, I shook my head in awe of *your* kind heart. You shared this story as if having such a close relationship with him was a given, like of course you loved your dad and thought he was the world's greatest dad. I didn't point out how most people don't react this way to their abusive fathers. Who was I to insert my negativity into your beautiful way of being? Instead, I let myself drift into your world. With eyes open, I kissed you, and your warmth dissolved my cynicism.

I learned many golden nuggets about you that night and in the following months. It took time to learn this stuff because you practiced the "art of silence" and didn't see the point in talking about your "stories." You were so modest and most everything about your past was a glowing achievement, so the stories had to be eased out of you delicately and in the right context. I'm sure, though, that there are countless other little miracles and juicy stories you never revealed. (Such is the way of the superhero, right?)

You lived with your grandparents and were a shoulder for your mom to cry on until she married your stepdad, Tom, when you were twelve. I want to say you lost your innocence by being the "man of the house" your mom depended on during your formative years. But I can't, because you never did lose your innocence. Or did you?

After your mom remarried, you lived and worked on Tom's farm in the panhandle of Oklahoma, a short fifteen miles south of your grandparents in Kansas. A couple of years later your younger brother, Scott, was born. "The panhandle? What's that?" I asked naively. You didn't answer immediately, and I watched as you shredded bar napkins and proceeded to assemble the pieces into some mysterious shape. You pointed to the top part—that was Kansas. The middle section you said was Oklahoma, and the third blob was Texas. Well, whaddya know.

Oklahoma has a slivered off section that juts out from the rest of the rectangle, much like the handle of a pan. And so does Texas. I hadn't known. You spoke proudly of your panhandle and of the gusty winds, the endless wheat fields, and the fresh red earth. You called it your "shire." And I couldn't wait to see it one day.

I asked what a typical day in high school had been like for you because you mentioned that high school was when you first developed narcolepsy. You gave me the rundown. It was no wonder you developed narcolepsy at that time. Your body needed sleep, John! Up for a run at 5:00 a.m., you hit the shower, ate breakfast, and drove off in your blue truck, down a dirt road to school. You had class till three. Then football practice: you were captain and led your team to win the Oklahoma State Championship three years in a row (details I found out upon further investigative questions). Okay, fine. Then after football practice each day—or depending on the season, 'cause you were also on the track and field team, the weight lifting team, the baseball team, and the basketball team (and had also won State every year in track and weight lifting—another detail I probed for)—you had band practice. You played the tuba. I had to pause you for a second: "Wait—hold up. So at football games, did you play in the game and also in the band at halftime?" I asked.

Of course you did. What was I thinking? It was nothing but a quick uniform switch. Then, after band practice, you had drama practice. If a play was being put on, you stayed late for rehearsal (because you were always the lead, and you'd also won multiple State awards and a national championship in this category, details I later learned from your mom). But on a typical day, after drama practice you moved along to choir practice; singing of course, was another one of your gifts. Then you went home and did homework. But because of your narcolepsy, reading made you fall asleep. To stay awake you developed a handy technique of reading while walking, and that's how you got your homework done. Then it was lights out at around 1:00 or 2:00 a.m., only to get up a few hours later, head out for your run, and start the whole thing all over again. Whoa John, what the hell?

"How—? Why'd you do all that?"

"To whom much is given, much is expected," you said.

"Where would you ever get such a preposterous idea?" I asked.

"The Book of Luke."

The nuns in elementary school had pounded it into your head. You'd been given a lot of gifts and people were counting on you. If you squandered the gifts God gave you, if you didn't live up to His potential for you, He, and everyone else, would be gravely disappointed. I guess with your big, trusting heart you'd innocently believed them and put down your video games and set to work to not disappoint anyone. Long after you'd left Christianity, these words were embedded in you like shards of glass.

Starting from an early age, wherever you went, people called you "special." They believed in you in a supernatural kind of way and expected from you accordingly. Inexplicably, you delivered. You were the quintessential golden boy, the town celebrity, the captain of the football team, the perfect Christian role model. Your name was known throughout the tri-state Oklahoma, Kansas, and Texas area. When I think of golden boys (in contrast to golden girls), I think of them as being so darn good and lovable you can't but help have a sweet spot for them. There's a reason they're usually everyone's favorite and the teacher's pet. I assumed/imagined all this reverence for you wasn't just because of your angelic good looks, boyish charisma, or hunky athletic abilities. No, it was because on top of all that, you were the kindest, most "good" person I'm sure they'd ever seen. Here's an example that proves my point: In one of our psych assessment classes, I had to ask you about the worst thing you'd ever done. After staring into the air and thinking for a long time, you finally found it. When you were a senior in high school, you asked a heavyset and unpopular girl to prom. What was the problem with *that*? I asked. You said you were mostly motivated by an inner desire to prove your faith in the Lord—like, how much could you demonstrate that you were his faithful servant? You felt this was wrong because you were being dishonorable and manipulative to the girl, like you had used her. You also added that the two of you had a damn good time and from then on became great friends. I rolled my eyes with a smirk. Please. Gimme a break, John. But I jotted it down, and did my little assessment report.

Once you were living in California, you tried to shed this "special" label. You thought being called special was simply people's projections of you, what they wanted to see. Yet the sticky thing—at least from my point of view—was that you played into their projections. You gave them evidence of being special. In journaling class, you once said you were "the greatest actor the world has ever known." I didn't believe you at the time and had no idea what you meant. How could you be acting? I felt your goodness and knew it to be true. There was no way it was an act. But regardless of what I thought, you wrestled internally with the burden of responsibility that people and family alike had placed on your shoulders. You did your damndest to live up to their expectations. You could not fail. A part of you must have also believed the myth; you once told me you knew that, no matter what you did, you were incapable of failing. As evidence of this, you told me how you once fell asleep at the wheel while driving home in Oklahoma. Instead of waking up in the hospital, you miraculously woke up safely in your car, two towns and twenty miles later. A part of you felt your success was somehow guaranteed, and no matter what, you would be protected.

You also used this "special" persona to keep you from being human and avoid the messiness that comes along with it. As long as you were golden and special, you thought, you wouldn't get hurt or do any of the hurting. For this reason, you waited to lose your virginity, thinking the longer you were a virgin, the closer you would be to God (this is also a conservative Christian idea, right?). Even though you had tons of girls after you—especially, I imagine, when you were touring as a lead singer in that college country Christian rock band (what was the name again?), singing to throngs of screaming fans. You ignored them. Sex was for everyone else, not you. The fact that you didn't have it kept you apart from your humanness. And, again, made you special.

But once you had untangled your beliefs about Christianity through inundating your brain with Eckhart Tolle and Byron Katie and moved to California and away from the community who believed you were special, you wanted to experience your humanness more fully. At twenty-seven, you lost your virginity to an older woman in Berkeley. By the time we got together, I was your third partner.

When you first shared your confusion about being called special, I didn't quite get the extent of this "special" complex, how huge it was, how you were like a celebrity back at home. I didn't understand the extent of the angst it caused you. I looked at you squarely and told you I didn't care who you were back where you came from or what everyone there thought. None of that had relevance to how I saw you. I adored you for you: your beautiful goodness.

I once asked you as we cuddled in bed: How was it you were unusually kind and understanding and loving toward all people all the time? How did you do it? What was your secret? Remember your response? It was plain and simple.

"I remember what it's like from before we got here. I never forgot what it feels like . . . that we're not separate."

"Hmm," I wondered, "but John, how is it that *you* didn't forget, but the rest of us have?"

Your eyes looked at me, full of innocence. You didn't know.

We could not have had more opposite upbringings. At the bar, after you shared parts of your childhood with me, I shared my darkest secrets with you—the ones no one, except family and a few long-time, trusted friends knew. From a young age, I had struggled with depression. Unlike you, I guess I forgot rather early on what it felt like before I got here. Or maybe I remembered all too clearly, and it was the contrast between the worlds that made me depressed.

As a little five-year-old, living in a thirty-floor Manhattan apartment building with twelve hundred other people and at least two hundred cats and dogs, I used to lie awake at night in my bottom Formica-white bunk bed, surrounded by a community of stuffed animals and Cabbage Patch Kids I could never quite talk to. My younger sister, Mila, slept peacefully above me, and this made me nervous. How could she fall asleep and I couldn't? I'd call her name, hoping she was awake so I wouldn't feel so alone and strange for still being awake. The bright light from the hallway cast a harsh glow over my bed and I tried to relax to the sounds of the distant television. Every night, it took me hours to fall asleep. Quiet tears soaked my pillow as I thought about death. Where did we go when we didn't exist anymore? I pictured a never-ending dark void and in it I floated alone for eternity. No one was there. Everyone I knew was gone. I was sad I would never see anyone I loved again. The image of forever haunted me, scaring me into insomnia; it was pure darkness. The endlessness trapped me. There was no way out. I'd be stuck in the dark. Forever. I tried to understand: if I were to die and be suspended in nothingness, how could I still be me, but dead? I clutched my pillow for safety. If I had never been born as me would I still exist, or would someone else have been born as me? These thoughts about death, these mazes of unknown possibilities, and the inevitability of my own vanishing self followed me as I peered out at the world. I've always lived my life in juxtaposition to death.

When I was seven and Mila was five and you were climbing trees with Luke in your grandparents' Kansas backyard, something strange started happening in my family. No one told me what happened, though, until years later, when the damage had been done and its shadow clung to me. One day after school, while I was talking on the phone, Mila covered her head in a plastic bag and supposedly tried to die. Whether she was intentionally suicidal or not is still unclear. But her actions were interpreted this way. She'd recently started first grade at our highly competitive Jewish parochial school and was depressed because we were expected to read and write in Hebrew as well as English, and she couldn't, due to an undiagnosed learning disability.

I didn't know about her suicide attempt and my parents didn't tell me until about three years later. By that point I had grown livid with both Mila and my mom because no matter what I did, Mila was inexplicably and overtly favored, and I was blamed for every fight and every little thing that went wrong. I never understood why. The injustice drove me to withdraw behind my bedroom door and immerse myself in schoolwork. At school, I channeled my anger on the basketball court.

Secrets, death, religion, and dogma hovered over my house. While you were out in the wheat fields growing up far away in the clutches of fundamentalist Christianity, I squeezed into crowded cross-town buses, choking for air underneath the weight of Orthodox Judaism. How did we make our way through? I attended a strict Jewish school (or *yeshiva),* kept kosher, and attended synagogue every Saturday in the right *shabbos* outfit or else. I had no outlet for freedom or creativity. Nobody saw me or got me. I grew up unseen. My dad was out of town on business most of the time, and my mom took my quietness personally and stressfully attended to Mila and my newly born sister, Leah. I had no one to cry to, no one who understood me, and no one who could coax me out of my quiet, shy shell. My parents insisted my problem was I was jealous of Mila. How does a ten-year-old convey to her parents that she's not jealous of her sister, but rather of the way her parents *treat* her sister?

In high school, I used to brood in a corner of the third-floor lounge. Wearing my long skirt uniform, listening to Smashing Pumpkins in my headphones, and watching the world through a thick layer of glass, as if life were an exhibit in a museum. I wanted to understand people, make sense of what I saw around me—the thousands of people rushing by, the mysterious building lights staring back at me through my bedroom window. I thought that if I could just get inside their heads and know what they were thinking, then I could figure out who I was, how I was supposed to be in the world, and what the purpose of my life was. And in the loneliness of my bedroom, squirming on my turquoise carpet as if trying to molt into something else, I agonized about not being able to live up to my potential. I wanted to reach within, grab my core, and extract it so badly. But I had no idea what was in there and I couldn't feel it.

I did what any good Jewish, Talmud-scholar-by-day, growing-up-in-the-big-city girl would do: clubs, drugs, withdraw, and rebel. And while you, John, were practicing tackles on the football field and out earning your state championship patches for your jacket, I was earning a reputation as the "druggie girl." It was only marijuana and the occasional ecstasy at raves, but since it was a yeshiva, after all, it was a big deal. At an early age I'd heard that we only use 10 percent of our brain, and I wanted to know what the other 90 percent was like. I thought drugs could show me. I'm not sure they did, but for better or worse they did help me get inside myself, explore around, and express a bit more than I could have otherwise.

After high school, I deconstructed the force-fed beliefs in Judaism, turned to the more mystical unseen forces that go by no particular name, and cultivated my own unique relationship to spirituality. I studied parapsychology, occult studies, mysticism, Taoism, Kabbalah, and Rastafarianism, to name a few. I crossed off bucket-list activities like bungee jumping, surfing, yoga, belly dancing, African dance, tai chi, capoeira, samba, and meditation. I danced at raves, clubs, festivals, streets, beaches; I danced at Rainbow Gatherings. I quested for the perfect beach, backpacked through Europe, the Bahamas, and Jamaica. I slept on a street bench with a homeless man in New York. I dropped out of NYU to follow love and lived in a crack house in North Carolina. I've done enough LSD to make me certifiably insane and chased my demons to hell and back dozens of times. I lived and worked as a yoga teacher in Rio de Janeiro and a kindergarten teacher in Tel Aviv. I made it my mission to find a way to be happy, to find my calling in life, and to live up to my potential. But still, what was it?

My major in college was individualized study; I designed a concentration called "People and the Universal Human Essence," and explored sociology, religion, philosophy, literature, and art from a myriad of cultures around the world. I compared and contrasted them and distilled their similarities down to a human essence. And you know what I found? You. You, John, are that essence.

Over the years I worked odd jobs ranging from receptionist, ghostwriter, yoga teacher, cocktail waitress, bartender, and internet sex chat-room hostess to nanny and ESL and kindergarten teacher. I hunted in all of them for my reason for being here, for a career, for a life I could love the rest of my days.

After starting and stopping on many different paths, by age twenty-five I felt pressure to have landed on a "solid career path," know what the heck I was doing with my life, and be earning the right kind of salary. Most of my friends and peers were either in graduate programs or established in relatively high-paying jobs. They seemed to know what they wanted to do with their lives. I felt I was lagging behind. It was then that I found something to combine several of my interests: working with kids, helping people, and physical movement. Becoming a pediatric occupational therapist seemed like a good enough fit, and I committed to the extensive prerequisite courses and applied for financial aid to attend the NYU master's program. I felt relieved that I would eventually have a "real job" and could finally participate in society as a "real person" with a decent income, not as the fuckup I felt I was.

On day one of the master's program, I had a feeling this was wrong, but I ignored it and shoved my face into my anatomy and physiology and neuroscience textbooks. The classes were tedious, and my classmates were type A women who wasted much of our class time freaking out about the material and drilling the professors about test questions weeks before the exam. The content was mindless but required endless memorization. As fall crept into winter, I hated myself for being in this unsure, depressed position yet again, and hated my life. Between my loans, the year and a half I had already invested in the prerequisite work, and the pressure I felt to have a real job and be like everyone else, I felt like a failure, trapped. I couldn't let myself abandon this career choice. I'd committed to this path and I'd have to suck it up and just do it. I didn't see any way out.

You've told me winters in Oklahoma are pretty severe, but winters in New York are a wicked possession of one's bones. I was living on the Lower East Side with Mila. She had recently gotten engaged. Each day was a miserable replica of the previous one, where I sat at my desk for hours upon hours and memorized information that lacked any meaning for me. I cried myself to sleep every night. I felt defective, unlovable. I retreated further into my detached world and lost touch with the everyday things I'd once enjoyed that had helped keep me grounded here. I had tried so hard, for so long, to find my joy, but instead a deep depression set in and wouldn't move.

My body went through the motions while my mind and heart were vacant. I no longer wanted to live in this world. It was too dark, too cold, and I couldn't see any future that was different from the pain I felt. Night after night, sleep relieved me of my tears, and I prayed never to wake up again. But each morning, fear knifed me in the stomach as I woodenly got up to face another day of grey, wondering why I hadn't just died in my sleep.

I waited at lights, crossed the streets, rode buses, stepped on the subway, and trudged through the day-to-day routine, alone and bundled up against the freeze in my long, black, puffy coat. Through my trance, I thought about death and the end of my life.

There are two kinds of people in this world: those who hit rock bottom and consider suicide. And those who don't. I'm the former.

Hope drained from me, leaving me numb. I felt nothing for other people and couldn't feel anything from them—not their love, not their concern. Nothing. I had returned to the world I'd known since childhood, a place at the edge of life and death where laughter is a strange echo I don't recognize and it feels like I'm neither here nor there. An in-between world where I don't know where home is. It's a dangerous edge to wander; one slip and it's over. Most people, wisely, avoid it at all costs.

You once told me your life was like a "bed of roses" and you'd never been depressed. How could that be? I guess the Golden Boy-Christian Disciple-Quarterback was busy with other things.

Something wasn't right; something was wrong with me. My mind was dark, my body numb, and my heart shut down. I couldn't just "choose" to fix it and choose to be happy, like some people suggested. Exercise would not extract this toxin. Therapy didn't help; in fact, it made it worse. All I wanted was the pain to end. I was tired of trying. My journey through life so far had exhausted me. I was alone in the in-between world. No one could see me there and no one could save me. I had tried to avoid this netherland, but nothing had worked out the way I'd hoped and intended. I couldn't try anymore. I just wanted to go home. Return to a place of warmth, ease, and pure love. You know that longing.

Shadows from the street flickered across my empty apartment. Mila was away, and I didn't bother turning on the lights. I walked to the kitchen, to the Xanax in the cabinet, and stood there watching the shadows. I opened the bottle, grabbed a large handful of pills, and swallowed them down with water. Feeling nothing, I headed to bed. No one would miss me. They'd probably be better off.

I wrapped my head in my blanket and smothered my face with my pillow, cutting off my air supply. I didn't have the guts to go all the way on my own, but I was ready to leave. I hoped that if I set up a conducive enough situation, death would meet me halfway. I remained motionless under the hot blankets, lest I take in air. My heart beat rapidly with fear. I prayed for a quick end, for the lights to go out, to wake up somewhere better, soon. The darkness fell.

But death never came for me. The following day, I was stirred awake by Mila. The Xanax still had its effect but as the room came into focus, hopelessness hit me again. I was scared to still be alive. Mila found the bottle of pills by my bed and phone calls were made. I had tried. I guess it wasn't my time.

In the months that followed, I felt I was having an existential crisis every minute of the day. Sitting at the edge of my bed, I gripped my head to stabilize my mind as it cycled through shrieks of anxious thoughts and terror about my future. I needed to know what I was going to do with my life, and I needed to know immediately. My sense of failure paralyzed me. I forgot who I was. Would I ever regain my will to live? I had lost interest in everything. What did I like, let alone love, about life? Where did I belong? My therapist was on-call for these attacks. It was decided that I needed to take a leave of absence from the OT program. I never returned.

They call this the quarter-life crisis and I was supposedly part of a "betwixt and between" generation. I don't know. With the help of family and friends, I finally made my way back to the land of the living. I remembered who I am. I surrendered to whatever I could find: a job teaching kindergarten in Tel Aviv after Mila's wedding in Israel. My path took me to a spiritual teacher in Jerusalem, which led me to transpersonal psychology in California, and finally to you. On that course, I found my direction, a calling of sorts, and in the process I found my joy again. Once I arrived in California, I felt my life had taken a change for the better; life was brighter, easier. Though there had been a couple of men in between, you helped me know love and warmth again. John, your presence continued to heal scars from the night I tried to die.

As I shared this with you at the bar that night in Mountain View, your eyes filled with understanding. You gathered me in your arms and whispered in my ear how grateful you were for my courage to share this with you and for having the strength to endure through it all. I felt closer to you than I'd ever felt to anyone. The love was palpable, filling the whole restaurant. The bartender told us how rare and refreshing it was to see two people so beautiful and loving toward one another. She served us champagne on the house. Now that you were with me, the ordinariness of my life had gone away, and I could finally trust that everything would work out for the best.

You once said that one of the reasons you were with me was that I helped you be more human. Ironic, isn't it? You said I showed you the swing of things, helped you get organized and grounded, and helped you begin to realize it was okay to express your real feelings. Who was saving whom?

John, I love you like the sky, forever and back, and forever again and again.

Your beauty fills me with tears. I can't hold them back.

Eternally,
Sarah

Dear John,

I'm anxious and scared to write this next part. Itching, fidgeting, and procrastinating. I swept my bathroom floor from the haircut I gave myself. My nails are bitten down to the quick. The coffee mug by my side is empty. I don't know if I can do it. People have called me courageous for writing to you and going back into my mind, reliving everything. I don't know if I have the courage to write anymore. I'm scared of how I'll feel as I delve. But I can't avoid it. It's too essential. Okay, John, here I go. Slowly. Letter by letter.

That night in November, we said goodbye and got off the phone. I fell into a dark, thick, dreamy sleep. Somewhere, my cell phone was vibrating. The sound was far away and I couldn't move to get it. It was still vibrating a few minutes later; I rolled over and picked it up. Your housemate Barbara was on the other end.

"Sarah honey," she said in her stern English accent.
        "Uh, yeah?" I croaked.
        "John has put himself in front of a train," she said.

It took me a second to understand.

"Oh my god," I cried, bolting up and straight into my blackened closet, throwing on a brown sweater and moccasins.

"He's still alive, but we're going to the hospital soon. Why don't you come over and we'll go together."

"Oh my god," I repeated. Shock had smacked me in the face.

My mind fractured. This was not possible. *You? John.* You, of all the people in the world, could not have put yourself in front of a fucking train. How could you do that? You'd never mentioned anything, ever, about death. But a part of me recognized this place somehow, as if it were an old dream from childhood. Your yearning for something else, somewhere else, had been there all along. I had felt it but consciously missed it.

I ran out the back door and the dark morning wind hit my face. Helicopters chopped loudly in the sky, searching the ground with their menacing spotlights. Were they looking for you? Strange coincidence that they were there, as if a hellstorm had been summoned in the night, rippling through the palm trees filling the air with dread. "Welcome to your very own nightmare," it said. I slammed on the ignition and my heart leapt through the windshield.

I drove with glazed eyes and reached the red light at Castro Street by the train station. The gates at the train tracks, your train tracks, were down. I was forced to wait for the train to pass, my first confrontation with it. How dare you, I seethed at the oncoming lights. The train glared back, bells and whistles screaming as its force of steel rushed by without mercy.

Your house was dark, but activity whispered in the air. Barbara was in the kitchen brewing fresh sage tea. I collapsed in an oversized armchair in the living room. Jean shuffled through papers on the dining room table and found your note. It was next to two checks—one made out to your dad for two hundred dollars and one to Barbara for a thousand dollars. We assumed you were paying your dad money he'd loaned you while leaving the remains of your account to Barbara. A scary chill filled the room. How long had you known?

Barbara read the letter out loud. I covered my face with my hands. Soft sobs escaped from my throat. Reality cracked. The atmosphere thickened and split into pieces. I was spinning. What if I never saw you again? My world was coming undone. I wanted to see you. I wanted to follow you wherever you were, into madness, wherever; I didn't care. What kind of a pain leads you to the train tracks on a cold November morning?

The police found your phone near your body. They dialed "Mom" and woke her up in Oklahoma. She identified you and your address. They knocked at your door at 5:30 a.m.

They found your black sleep mask on the tracks. It was the same one you used to blindfold me for my surprise birthday dinner. Why did you bring it with you, John?

Barbara and I sat at the kitchen table, drinking the tea. And it was bitter. We reviewed every detail about the night before. The last person to see you was Malcolm, Barbara's son, at around midnight. His chore was to unload the dishwasher. You had helped him. That was your last documented activity: helping your housemate unload the dishwasher. Barbara and Jean had seen you earlier in the evening, about to leave the house in your yellow jacket. You were blurry-eyed and out of it. Suspecting something, they stopped you and wouldn't let you leave. They hugged you and told you they loved you. Then one of them saw you on the phone, talking with me. That's when they went to bed. They'd thought to make you sleep in their bed to keep an eye on you and make sure you were safe, but then they thought better of it, reasoning that they couldn't keep you like a prisoner. What if you needed to use the bathroom in the middle of the night? They weren't going to follow you like wardens.

I followed Barbara's white car to Stanford Hospital. We were a slow, sad caravan. The sun was coming up. But the air around me was grey, full of the suffering I'd always known was there. My eyes drooped as life was sucked from me. I prayed for you. Over and over, like a loop: "Hang in there, John. Hold on. Please. Please." Could you hear me?

Finally, we parked.

To enter the ER waiting room, we had to place our belongings on a stainless steel cart and go through metal detectors. Barbara and Jean unloaded books and newspapers as if they were waiting for a doctor's appointment. I couldn't fathom reading. The security guard joked with them about something or other. I turned away and watched the pale white sky through the wall of hospital windows. Detachment set in. Beneath my sweater and sweatpants, my bones huddled for warmth. I shivered. It was so cold. The air conditioning didn't help. We were finally granted admission (really? like we really wanted to be there) and allowed through the metal detectors.

The waiting room had brown walls, brown chairs, and a long, brown wooden magazine rack. The overhead lights were dim. I sat shivering and blank. A social worker named Michael came over and kneeled on the floor to talk to us. He spoke kindly of you, as if he were your friend and knew how special you were. I appreciated this softness. He told us we couldn't see you because there was too much activity in your room as teams of doctors and other hospital staff were going in and out. You were unconscious and in critical condition. Michael didn't tell us anything more.

A police officer interrupted my daze. He asked to speak with me, identifying me as your girlfriend. I didn't argue. We sat in a small space partitioned by brown curtains. He flipped on a digital recorder. Had you talked of suicide before? No. Had you used drugs? No. When did I see you last? Tuesday night. When had I spoken to you last? Last night. My voice creaked out, low and scratchy. He asked me to speak louder. I felt defective. I couldn't find energy to raise my voice, but I tried. When he was done, he asked if I had any questions.

"What happened?"

"All we know is that at around five fifteen this morning, John laid down next to the train tracks. Not on them. The conductor spotted him from a ways a way. John's body was shaking and convulsing. The conductor blew the horn loud and clear over and over again, but John didn't move. The conductor wasn't allowed to stop the train. John's leg was hit and he was thrown on impact."

"How is he?"

"His leg was shattered," was all he said.

I joined Barbara and Jean back at our spot. The cop's news was somewhat reassuring. If your leg was the only damage, then that was okay. You could pull through that. Barbara got up to take a phone call from your dad in Texas.

"Is it just me or is it fucking freezing in here?" I said to Jean.

"It's just you," Jean said handing me her shawl.

I bundled up but was still cold, and I shivered as sheaths of terror sliced through me. I was powerless to stop them.

Where were you? We waited.

I made a phone call to my coworker at my practicum site. Speaking the words out loud on the phone made everything more real. I couldn't hold back the sobs. I managed to say I couldn't come in that day because I was at the hospital. But I didn't tell her why. I was hoping you would make it through and I wanted to protect your privacy, just in case.

Barbara came back and reported the latest update from your dad, who was on his way to the airport. All your limbs were shattered. Your internal organs were damaged and bleeding. This news shook me. *Oh god*, I cried. Was this true? Your beautiful, strong body no longer intact? Your body had warmed my cold and melted me like no other. Bleeding inside. What was happening? What was real anymore?

Laura, the next social worker on duty, emerged from behind the swinging doors. Michael's graveyard shift had ended and he'd gone home; just another day's work. She led us to a small, private, windowless room, deeper within the bowels of the hospital. The staff wanted (or needed) to give us more privacy, Laura said; you were the most serious case in there. Fear followed me and my body couldn't stop shivering. This private waiting room was claustrophobic and stored broken hospital furniture: an old utility cart and half a lamp lay discarded in the corner. The other part of the room contained a brown love seat, a side table with a lamp, a chair, and a beige wall phone. This is where Laura told us what no one had dared mention earlier: your brain was bleeding. They were taking you upstairs for surgery. This was now the fourth blow to my system about your status.

I leaned over. My insides squeezed, I could hardly hold my body upright. I couldn't sit still; I couldn't stay in that room. I had to get back out to the other waiting room, as if waiting in the room designated for less fatal emergencies would change things back to when you just had a shattered leg. Barbara was on the beige wall phone, making calls. There was no cell phone reception in this room. In that instant, I needed to talk to my mom. Immediately. I stumbled through a maze of nurses' desks, past curtained emergency stations, and back out through the swinging doors to the brown waiting room. I dialed my mom; she was in Israel. The phone rang and rang and rang. No one answered. The time difference was ten hours. I called again. No one was there. I called my dad in New York.

"Where's mom? I need to talk to mom," I cried.

"Sarah. What happened?" he asked. "Are you okay? Sarah. What happened?" His voice was already in New York crisis mode.

I tried to speak but couldn't. Wails, sounds I'd never heard come out of me, flew from my throat.

"I'm—I'm at the hospital," I finally managed. Tears and mucus covered my face.

"Sarah, what happened?"

"John's—attempted suicide—oh god . . . he was hit by a train. Oh god. Oh god. They don't know if he's going to make it." I sobbed uncontrollably. The more I said it out loud the more I couldn't hold it in anymore. My whole body heaved and I cried, oblivious to the other people in the room.

"I'm calling your mother on the other line. Hang on, talk to Leah."

I spoke to my sister Leah for a second and then my mom called on the other line. Another bout of sobbing hysteria flooded me as I tried my best to tell her what happened.

When I got off the phone, Laura touched me gently on the shoulder. "Sarah, do you have a support system?"

I nodded weakly. "Yeah, but I don't want to call them yet—to protect John's privacy."

"Sarah." She looked me straight in the eyes. "We need to worry about you now. You need to call your support system. And you need to call them now."

That's when I knew. It was all over. You were gone. My body collapsed in a chair and my cries filled the room. It was all I could do to not fall on the ground and beg to be swallowed up by the hole that had opened.

"John just passed in surgery. I'm so sorry." She put her arms around me. Sadness poured from my eyes, my nose was dripping. The room blurred and refracted through my tears. How could you? How could you go and die? How could you leave me so alone and terrified?

There was nothing left to do. Somehow my legs moved and walked me to the small waiting room. I huddled between Barbara and Jean on the loveseat for warmth, in shock; their bodies held me up as we waited for your doctors to come down and talk with us. We waited in the cold room for forty-five minutes. I struggled to stay conscious. I wanted to sleep and never wake up.

It felt like an eternity had passed by the time the doctors finally arrived. Their mouths moved with clinical information but what they were actually saying was unknown to me. I tried to pay attention but soon hung my head and gave up, too weak to hold its weight anymore. What difference did any of it make? You were gone.

We were given permission to see your body. It was upstairs. Somehow, we changed locations. I couldn't do it though. I didn't want the image of your crushed body ever in my mind. I stayed in the waiting room, the third one of the day. Barbara and Jean sat with your body until the coroner came to take it.

It was then that I was left alone. I sat by myself in a brown vinyl-cushioned chair staring blankly at the floor, weeping, in a freezing hospital in California, thousands of miles away from home. At the time, it didn't register how deserted I felt. A hospital volunteer kept watch over this waiting room from behind a desk. Every so often she cast me fearful glances that seemed to say that my uncontrollable crying was scaring people. I was the poster child of everyone's worst-case scenario. Compared to what it appeared I was living through, the situations that had brought them to the hospital that day—surgeries, procedures, etc.—seemed relatively manageable. No one wanted to be in my shoes.

And then my phone started ringing. I hadn't had service for the past hour while in the small waiting room. My mom couldn't reach me and had panicked. There were nine messages from her. My dad and sister Mila were already at JFK and on their way to San Francisco. My dad had called the head of my school and told them to find me and make sure I had support. James Stone, the dean of my school, had called several times. He wanted to see me as soon as I was done at the hospital. The word was spreading quickly, and with much terror. I had to get out of there and stop waiting.

I searched the hallways for Barbara and Jean. I couldn't find them. I asked the hospital volunteer to look for them. She disappeared for a long time. I couldn't take being in the hospital for another minute. I did my best to find the elevator, stumbled through the building in a stupor, lost and disoriented. Eventually I fell out of the automatic sliding doors and into the outside world.

Like a dream or scene from a movie, objects and people moved past and then disappeared. My feet didn't register the concrete beneath them. While I'd sat shivering in the air-conditioned hospital, the weather outside had become hot and sunny, like a perfect summer day in July. I looked up at the sky into the expanse of space far away and felt you flying free as your warmth exploded through the world below. The change in weather was extraordinary. How you must have soared that day. I can't imagine your sense of freedom. But I could feel it in the air. And for the first time that year, flocks of birds ready to migrate south flew in graceful formations, back and forth throughout the sky. They reminded me of how you danced.

Somehow I found the parking lot and my car. I paid the parking fee. Somehow I drove the car to school. The dean met me at the entrance. The administration stood hushed, waiting for me.

A box of blue tissues by my side, I cried through the events of the morning, trying to explain what happened as best as I could. How do you explain what happened when you just don't know what happened? I shared my version of it: the narcolepsy, the breakdown, the sleep deprivation, the anxiety, the depression. I blamed myself for not doing more to help you. Had I only been there with you last night, had I only gotten the Ambien in the mail in time, I could've helped you get a night's rest. If you had just gotten a night's sleep, you would've been okay. You had a psychiatrist appointment at 10:00 a.m. that very day (couldn't you have just held on till then??) and you would've gotten help.

"Sarah, you can wrestle with what you could have done to save him, but I will wrestle with *you*. And we can have this wrestling match over and over again. There was nothing more you could have done. This was not your fault," James said.

I didn't believe him yet.

I don't know how I got myself home. A flock of birds flew through the sunny sky. Time slowed down. My car moved in slow motion. My neighborhood, full of royal palm trees, looked dead and muted. I was frozen, unsure what to do, how to live.

Sophie was driving back and forth up my street, looking for me. It was a meager comfort to see her through the car window. We both parked. We sat on my porch steps. Minutes later, Francesca walked up. The three of us sat in quiet shock in the unseasonably warm November weather. A train went by in the distance. I began to tell them what had happened.

The afternoon was spent huddled in my apartment with the blinds drawn, all of us no longer sure of the world around us. We held hands and cried for you, our unique, beautiful friend. We tried to piece it all together, but words spent were futile. How could you—someone so loving, so big-hearted—destroy yourself in such a violent, public way?

The day you left, I died. Everything I'd ever known to be true, everything I knew of myself and about life, was officially gone.

Take this for now, John, it's the best I can do. That day at the hospital was the worst day of my life. And if somehow I could erase it from my memory, I wouldn't. I have to hold on to all I've got of you. Even my nightmares.

I love you.
Sarah

....

Dearest Family and Friends

Please forgive me for my lack of willingness to face this season of my life I don't know how to say goodbye I don't need to say goodbye if I can just take on the power of your love for me. I don't need to do this I don't know why my mind isn't capable of understanding.

I love you mom DAD Grandpa Jim Grandma Cynthia Scott Luke Stephanie Jack and Dianne, Brandon SARAH BEN Brett Richard Olivia Mckendra Barbara Jean Anthony Malcolm Sophie

Somehow I have to believe that there is some original innocence within that transcends all. The support that I have had from all of you is more than anyone could dream hope for

I'll be entering back into spirit for another round to fully embody myself the self, I can only imagine what this cost will be to you The cost that I imagine me living as a coward seems much greater as well ~~you~~

~~now I have the bigg~~

~~Are all so able to move past this knowing that~~

I wish I could take this all less seriously

~~I will do my best~~

because it is and what if I could embrace this lack of seriousness and embrace each of you

51

I can't bear the thought of me in a mental institution until they put me out on the street

And the biggest part is feeling so ashamed of who I am while you have to have this in your life.

John,

Our time together was as warm and simple as a sunny, green park. For a while there, we made out endlessly in your car like teenagers. Your car was our sweet bubble of innocence. We were that couple that always had an arm around one another, held hands, or embraced while having a conversation. I know it took you a while to get used to showing affection at school, but eventually you got over it. If we were within a few feet of each other, it was almost impossible not to touch each other.

In the evenings, after spending a few hours doing schoolwork together, we drank red wine on my couch or sipped straight from the bottle while sitting on benches in the downtown Palo Alto moonlight. You showed me your love of red zinfandels. Huh? You were a red wine connoisseur—another surprising tidbit in the mystery that was John—from Oklahoma. And in our red wine reveries, I loved taunting you with challenging truth-or-dares, like the time I dared you to nonchalantly walk outside to the curb wearing nothing but a towel and wave to my elderly Polish neighbor, Maria, who spent most of her time sitting on her front porch.

Everything we did, no matter how mundane, was imbued with a special grace. Changing my duvet cover together felt like a childhood game. A trip to the supermarket became an innocent adventure. Remember the night at Whole Foods spending hours lost in the different sections, sampling pastries and cheese and chatting with the people who worked there? That was yummy, John, better than any fancy date in some shmancy restaurant. God, and we used to dance *all* the time. Everywhere, and at any opportunity; in my bedroom as we got dressed in the mornings, in my bedroom as we celebrated the end of the day, in my black-and-white-checkered kitchen, in parking lots, Burger King, clubs, at dawn by the eucalyptus trees . . . wherever music played, we were sure to move to it together. And then we took those delightful ballroom dance lessons Friday nights at the community center. We were the youngest couple there. The men were supposed to rotate around the circle and switch partners, but we never let go of one another. Holding your hand was all I needed; it was my passport to your magical world. I could have been anywhere—a slum, airport, garden, wedding, or funeral—and as long as your hand was in mine, there was a force between us that made everything okay. Not just okay, but transcendent.

I love how at 8:00 a.m. on my birthday, just a few weeks after we got together, you disassembled my kitchen window screen and climbed through with bags of groceries and an orange rose because my roommate forgot to leave the door unlocked for you, as was planned. With a knock on my bedroom door, you surprised me in bed with homemade blueberry pancakes, maple syrup, juice, and tea. This seriously made me question your origins. I mean, come on. What planet were you from? How you managed to clang around in the kitchen without waking me was beyond me. I did, literally, ask you several times where you came from. You laughed your deep, sunny laugh and replied that you loved surprising the people in your life. Lying tangled and wrapped in my white, fluffy blankets, we skipped class and stayed in bed. You called it "a little slice of heaven."

Thank you for showing me.

Forever,
Sarah

P.S. Oh, and one more thing. Our naps! Remember our little naps together in your car?! You'd take naps in your car throughout the day to manage your narcolepsy. When I first learned about this I thought you were so hardcore, and then you took me for one and I grew to love them. Your car was a meditative cocoon you had conditioned from hours and hours of driving in blissed-out states while listening to Eckhart Tolle or Byron Katie. It was where you mastered a state of pure peace and felt the "aliveness of every cell in your body." Your car had a clean, freshly vacuumed smell, kind of like a new gymnasium smell. A high school picture of your brother, Scott, rested on the dash and an om sign was pasted on the rearview mirror. A midday nap in this space was a relaxing refuge, like floating in the sky. We extended the seats flat; you offered a pillow for my neck, a blanket, and an eye pillow. It was so adorable that you napped with an eye pillow. You set your phone for fifteen minutes, and we lay back in the stillness and peace. You guided me to bring awareness to my eyelids and feel the heaviness of them. Your words petered out, and soon you were asleep. I drifted as I bathed in your presence. Sharing this secret naptime ritual felt like innocent, childlike love, and it became a part of us as we walked back to class hand in hand like two curly-haired kindergartners.

Dear John,

So you must know the suffering and pain I've felt his past year. You've seen how hard I've tried, how I've worked through my grief. I've plumbed the depths of hell looking for you. I've moved through the boundaries of reality searching for you, desperately trying to find ways to feel you and be with you again. I don't know if I've found you. I want to join you. My feelings for you haven't changed now that you aren't in your body. They've grown.

When I returned from the hospital, I felt an urgent need to see you. Immediately. I could not. In my shocked state, a twisted knowing in my stomach told me it wasn't possible. Not. Ever. Going. To. Be. Possible. My mind swam, trying to adjust to this new fact. Fingers curled like claws, I wanted to drop to the floor and throw a tantrum and exact immediate gratification—to see you again, that instant. I festered on this impossibility as if it were a sleight-of-hand trick: if I could only crack the magician's code, you would suddenly appear—your angelic face intact, looking handsome in my favorite blue-and-navy-striped shirt. When would I see you again?

The answer hissed at me and echoed through my mind. *At my death.* "You have to be the first person I meet when I die." It became a prayer. A desperate one. *Please be the first person I see the second I die.*

My skin scrawled, the longing coursed through me. I couldn't believe I wasn't going to see you for at least fifty more years. I couldn't wait another minute to see you. I ached for death, was desperate to break down death's door and join you. Now, with one foot in this world and one foot in yours, I wait for my admittance. I wait restlessly for this body to drop so I can be with you again.

Your sudden, self-inflicted death rattled my mind completely, like the circuits of my brain were blown out. I couldn't comprehend what you'd done. That you were gone. Dead. The permanency of what you did was incomprehensible, sending me into a vortex of sheer fear and pain. Beyond words.

And you left voluntarily. You left me behind. Left me here. To do what? What was I to do without you? What could be worth doing without you? Your suicide destroyed any sense of meaning I'd ever pieced together to help me navigate the world. The day you left me, everything I'd ever known to be true or real crashed down. And I say this as someone who has thought about death since the age of five and even tried to take her own life once.

My biggest fear was never of spiders, failing a test, not having a date to prom, or flying. Since I was a little girl, my worst fear was of loving a man who would die before me, leaving me to live out the rest of my years without him. Every movie, book, and song I ever saw, read, or heard that told of this star-crossed fate moved me to inexplicable spells of weeping, like extrasensory empathy for these women. I didn't understand how these women survived the absence of their beloved. How do widows around the world survive the separation from their love? How do they find the will to live again after being stripped of a part of themselves? How do they ever learn to love again? How do I go on when my soul mate is dead? How do I survive? I don't feel I can. I struggle with this question every day.

There seems no worse a fate; with every man I ever fell in love with, I harbored secret panics about his death. A part of me felt the ache of losing you every time we were together, especially when you walked away from me as I stood on my street under a sprawling magnolia tree or when you were sick with a 102-degree fever. I feared you'd die and leave me. I was right. You must have known you would die early. Maybe it's why you struggled to commit to a future with me, with school, with your work. Maybe this was your destiny. Maybe.

When you left, you took my heart with you. Will I ever get it back? Do I even want it anymore, without you? When your soul left your body, mine went with it. Now I'm lost, looking for you, looking for myself, writing to you, hoping you'll answer me.

You ripped me apart. And ripped some more. Every inch of me bled, and bleeds still. I'm left to piece myself and my heart back together. But I don't have the strength or the will. How do I do this, John? Please help me. Please fucking answer me.

I don't want to live in the world without you. What I would give to see you again, even if just for a single second.

Yours always.
Sarah

Date: November 30, 2009
Subject: Treading in Hell

John,

After your death, Walter, our professor, approached me and offered to be the chairperson for my dissertation committee. His daughter had died the year before in a tragic car accident; he said he knew what I was going through, that most people wouldn't, and he would like to help me get through the next few years of school without any further obstacles. One of the first things he said to me was:

"Right now you are in hell. That's what it is. Pure hell. But there are many levels of hell; it goes down very deep. The trick is—you don't want to go so far down that you can't get out. You have to do whatever you can to stay within the upper levels of hell. You have to eat. You have to sleep. Try to exercise a little. Talk to people. Therapy. You have to do *whatever* you can to stay within the upper levels of this hell."

I tried my best. It was hard. I longed for death daily.

....

Dear John,

The days felt endless and blended into sleepless nights where even my Ambien didn't help. After a few hours of sleep, I'd wake in the middle of the night shocked anew, and sob silently in my bed until my tears began to soothe me and I could relax enough to feel the nearness of sleep. Waking up in the morning was grey, colorless, pointless. The day was dead to me.

I drove up and down El Camino, alone, listening to the radio as I searched for you through the shadows of places we'd been together: the bowling alley, Whole Foods, Jiffy Lube, all the different average-fare restaurants. Each moment we'd shared, regardless of how mundane, was a memory with no possibility of being replicated. Each love song I heard on the radio ripped open streams of tears. On freeways, I wanted to drop my head on the steering wheel and let my car crash into the cement barriers. I took so much of you and our time together for granted, thinking you'd always be here with me. I could've been a kinder, warmer person to you.

Your voice, your body, your hands are far away. They don't exist anymore. I'll never hear you sing again. I'll never hold your hand. I'll never see your blue eyes, except on perfect, sunny days when the sky is soft and the right shade of translucent blue. That's when my heart stops for a beat and I'm frozen in my tracks, remembering your eyes. But it's still not the same.

I had to reach you. I had to be with you again. I'd go anywhere to be with you. I wanted to follow you. I wanted to so badly. I had nothing left. I was falling under, deeper and deeper. I couldn't go on another day; I had no desire to.

The day after your memorial, the one we held for you, was the hardest point in my grief. The finality of your absence became real. Permanent. Irreversible. Cold like a crypt in winter. Pigeons swarmed outside my window in the icy wind. The pain was so thick I couldn't escape. I slumped over my desk, tears soaking my face. I begged you to come for me, to take me away and save me. Where were you? Where were you? I cried. My grip on life was slipping. I wanted to die. The pain was too sharp, I couldn't hold on anymore. I was too tired to care. Nothing mattered.

I lay in bed that night buried under thick blankets, crying. Alone. If Ben hadn't come in, I don't know if I would've made it through the night. He sat on my bed and held my hand in a tight grip that gave me strength to live through the night, to make it through one more day without you. Without his hand, I was too weak to go on. The pain was too unbearable to endure and continue to endure for the rest of my life. I couldn't do it without you. You'd given me warmth and love that softened the edges around my heart and around my life. Now that warmth had disappeared, only to be replaced with terror and darkness.

Ben held my hand, but you must have been holding my hand too. You were surely there, encouraging me to go on. The searing, firsthand knowledge of the unbearable pain that suicide inflicts on those left behind has been the only reason I haven't taken my life to join you in death. I could never knowingly cause this pain in anyone. It's too brutal for a human heart to bear. But if it weren't for this one awful truth, we'd be together now. You hadn't considered anyone's feelings (I have been there; I understand you were in a state of numbness, confusion, and constriction, and simply weren't capable), but my lesson had been learned. I refused and still refuse to cause this unbearable suffering in anyone's life. It's what's kept me alive. Even when my life feels like a straightjacket and I'm being held against my will, locked in a mental ward. Banging my head against the walls and screaming bloody fire at the top of my lungs, there's no way out.

Ben held me up when I couldn't hold myself. I guess that's how we get through and somehow survive the pain. I would've held you through yours, if only you'd let me.

I'm so angry I want to scream. I just want to hold your hand, RIGHT NOW.

But I can't.

Always,
Sarah

John,

Darkness descended early on that Sunday afternoon in February. I'd been huddled in the fetal position on the couch, missing you. My wet face was covered in dripping mucus. Hours passed this way. My chest was leaden with the ruthless pain and longing I couldn't bear anymore. In an instant, suddenly, like a cat pouncing an unseen insect, I became furious at myself for being trapped in my body and in my life, not able to do a damn thing to be with you. I wanted out. I wanted to get the fuck out of my body. You know that feeling. I wanted to get the fuck out of my life and have the nightmare end already. But I couldn't. There was nothing to do other than be with the goddamn pain.

I felt a need to exhale my venom in a stream of poison that would taint the world with how I felt. I needed to smoke. I'd quit smoking three years earlier, at age twenty-seven, when I'd moved to California. It was a habit I'd started when I was eighteen and had loved. While lying crumpled on the couch, the craving for a cigarette boiled in my blood. I wanted to feel the crisp burn of sucking smoke into my lungs. I needed to damage myself with my own anger. The very thought of it surged me with energy, and I stormed out of my apartment in a crazed rage. I could hardly see—my hair a mess, eyes swollen and lifeless from crying—as I dumped myself in my car, blasted whatever pop music was on the radio, and drove like the town witch to the nearest convenience store.

"Camel Lights," I muttered to the tall, heavyset Asian woman behind the counter wearing a grey, baggy sweatshirt. With pack in hand, I sped to an abandoned lot, out of place on a quiet residential street lined with white picket fences and loosely flowing yellow rose bushes. Navy blue darkness thickened the air. The plot looked like a ghostyard, overgrown with straggly weeds and a single weeping willow—perfect for my first cigarette of hate and rage. I climbed to the top of a large pile of brown, wet mulch and dead leaves and plopped down, basking in the filth. I inhaled my first cigarette and felt the woody, dirty smoke course through my chest. The poison settled my mind, just momentarily. As I exhaled roughly, my eyes narrowed wickedly and I glared through the night at the ghosts I couldn't see but knew were there. "Fuck you all," I hissed.

How did my curses feel, John? Probably nothing compared to what I was feeling. Or then again, maybe you felt what I felt. My sweatpants were soaked through, but I didn't give a shit about the mulch, the squirming bugs, or the dirt.

"AHHHHHHHHHHHHHHHHHHH," I screamed.

I was furious at my life, my fate, the universe. Like a little kid pinned down by a grown-up for a spanking, I was helpless, grasping for punches at the air, squirming for something to hit. I was met with nothingness; there was no one to attack. I hungered to grip the earth high above my head and smash it into the concrete ground, shattering all life into a million pieces. But with my moral constraints, the only target for my rage was myself. My long-forgotten, squashed, self-destructive tendencies roared back to life once again. I'd kept them quiet for many years, eliminating all drug use and smoking, trying to be a "good girl," seeking enlightenment or whatever, trying to be a woman worthy of you. But in that moment, I wanted to get fucked up—to blow out my mind with coke or something equally violent. I wanted to destroy something. I wanted to destroy myself. The structures in my mind I'd constructed or believed in to make sense of this world had collapsed the day you died. My point of view as I used to know it was gone; why couldn't the entirety of my self—body and spirit—go along with it? Maybe this is what your death march to the train felt like: destruction and explosion in a mass collision of steel, track, and body. Bang. How satisfying.

The unsatisfying reality was, I knew I wouldn't do anything. I still had self-control, and that was just as maddening. The most I could do was vent my anger by smoking and slowly killing myself. Breathing in fire and transforming the elements in my body to smoke empowered me. Sitting with my cold, damp legs sloped downward on my pile of dirt, I flicked my cigarette at the willow tree and prayed for an early death. After these spells of rage and grief moved through me, I usually collapsed into bed and fell asleep. I'd awake the next day and experience a vague, grey nothingness—a neutral holding space, like floating in a sensory deprivation chamber—as if my brain and body simply couldn't sustain any more pain; the circuitry had crashed itself and, as a result, had gone into standby mode. At first, this odd standby mode would be brief, maybe a day or two. Experiencing it, I felt strangely outside myself, like I was on my own personalized brand of antidepressant. I knew I wanted to grieve. I knew I felt sad. Yet it was like I didn't have juices left to feel those feelings anymore; the battery was dead.

This neutral state would then subside after a day or so and a new wave of grief would come barreling over me. Then, when I came up for air again, I'd be held over in another standby mode for another period, this time longer. The process continued this way for months. Each day was a different roller coaster ride of primal emotion. At around nine months, I began to reach a place where the waves were smaller and smaller and the holding periods became longer and longer. It was in these holding periods that I grew stronger, like a starved plant finally watered and expanding toward the sun. With each visit to hell, I returned with more strength than I'd ever known before. Often after a few rounds of grief and standby mode, I felt ferocious, like a tiger ready to fight. It continues to be this way.

I'm not sure my grieving will ever end. I'll miss you for the rest of my life. My wound is scarring but will never fully heal.

Yours,
Sarah

....

Dear John,

Tonight I feel so alone. It's dark and cold. Life has moved on. How do I go through all the years ahead of me without you? I still don't know. How do I go on loving you and missing you like this for the rest of my life? I can pretend my life has moved on. I can put things in motion, but underneath, my life doesn't go on without you. What you did ended me as I used to be. Now I'm stumbling blindly in the dark. There are no lights and no guides. Answer me. Please.

A few weeks after you died, Barbara gave me five of your journals, written over the years. The first one was from your college days when you were a devout Christian at Oral Roberts University. Barbara and Jean warned me that the final ones were about me, that you were deciphering your feelings for me. I didn't care. I had to know.

It was what was inside the marble black-and-white notebook I got you to write our goals and dreams for our future in that brought me to my knees. While sitting at my kitchen table, we wrote down our plans to work together as psychologists, write a book about love and relationships, and one day open a healing retreat center. You wanted it in New Mexico and I was thinking the Caribbean. When I saw the notebook again, "*#1 NY Times Bestseller*" was scrawled on the cover in your animated handwriting. The innocence of those words made my heart stop. Inside, only fifteen pages or so had been used. In one entry you wrote:

> *"It was very likely this December I would have been proposing to her on the slopes of New Mexico when we went to see my parents or in the spring on our anniversary date night at some place with palm trees out the wahzoo and singing the song 'It's a little bit funny, this feeling inside . . .' And my body would not, could not have it."*

I ignored the rest—the part where you processed your confusion about being with me. I reread the part where you contemplated proposing to me. Your plans were sweet, perfectly you, from the heart. My eyes blurred with disbelief. You'd planned on proposing. We could've married? Tears spilled onto the page. My insides filled with a sickly, bittersweet liquid, pulling me in every direction. How unfair to discover this future after you died and that this dream could never be anything more than an old journal entry found while looking for answers about your suicide.

There would be no curly-haired children to cuddle with under the covers. No quaint dinners by a fire with a bottle of red wine and you singing. No living in Oklahoma and watching football games with your mom. No working together, no joint practice, no books, no spiritual retreat center. No marriage proposal on a ski slope in New Mexico or in a palm tree grove in California. I would never again hear you sing "Your Song" or "I Just Called to Say I Love You." I lost a past and a future. You and I are frozen in time as we were.

I'm alone in missing the things about you that only I knew. No one I know has experienced this kind of loss. No one understands how much is lost. Not Barbara, not Jean, not my family, not my friends, not Brandon, not even your family; they have each other and a lifetime of your memorabilia.

Somehow I've got to believe there's a purpose for this, a reason this has happened, some kind of orchestrated plan. I must have a purpose for still being here, left behind. Why else am I here going through this? I've got to keep going. I've got to fulfill my purpose—whatever that may be. When my purpose in life is fulfilled, I'll be released and can join you. That's the only thing I want. I have to get through this life before I can reach my prize. I wait and work the hell out of my pain. I wish I could speed up the years and be with you now. Oh god. It's beyond heartache I feel. It's a soul ache that spreads through my abdomen and explodes through my chest. I want to be with you tonight. I would give anything to dance in your arms.

John, what do I need to do? Where am I?

I'm relieved that you're free, returned back to your source. My love wants what's best for you. How could I be the one to determine what that is? You're no longer suffering and in pain. That's what matters. It's my job to overcome my selfish need for you to have stayed for me in order to alleviate my fears and my pain about your death. I could never ask that of you. But a part of me deeply demands this and curses you for what you've done. How do I reconcile this? That the sweetest, most beautiful man I've ever known did the most painful, terrorizing act to me? How do I hate you when I idealize you so? This conflict pierces me in half and brings me to my knees over and over again.

I love you,
Sarah

the map:
guidance for despair

ACKNOWLEDGE AND SURRENDER

When you're in despair like this and your whole world has
fallen apart, there is nothing to do. There is nothing you can
do. Absolutely nothing will help alleviate the pain and shock.
Most people won't understand what you're going through
unless they too have survived a suicide of someone very close
to them. Even most professional therapists may not fully grasp
the type of pain you're in and the internal and external devastation left in the wake of suicide. I state this as fact and
truth as both a personal survivor and as a psychologist who's
worked with suicide survivors and in the suicide prevention
field. Unless you've gone through the suicide of a loved one
personally, the experience is unknowable. Surviving suicide is
qualitatively different than other kinds of grief and loss. It's a
specific brand of darkness and terror that is all-encompassing
and blinding. Truly dark and unfathomable. Earth-shattering
devastation and desperation. The only thing to do in this stage
is to feel the pain and to cry and scream and kick and rage and
let it out. Acknowledge your despair, welcome it and be with

it. Allow the despair and the sorrow to be exactly as it is. Cry, cry, and then cry some more.

GATHER COMMUNITY SUPPORT

There's something inherently sacred and private about utter sadness and the depths of this pain that can truly only be experienced by you. But please don't do this by yourself. Having another person there mitigates how deep you can go into your pain. This is a good and a bad thing. Sometimes you need to go deep down into that underground hell that only you know. It's not fun—in fact, it sucks more than anything—and yet going there and grieving in that lonely, despairing place is ultimately what will help you navigate out. But sometimes you need to be with others.

If you have friends or family that can hold you—physically hold you, like you're a baby—while you're crying uncontrollably, that can be one of the best ways to be with despair. I never had anyone hold me, and yet I know it's what I truly needed. As I wrote in one of the emails in this section, when Ben came into my room and held my hand through one of my darkest nights, that in itself helped carry me through.

Do not go through despair alone. DO NOT. Make sure you are surrounded by people who love you. Be in community. Ask to be held. And do this as often as you can. No one will know what to do or say to help you right now. You can tell them what you need. You need to be held. You may also need someone to help clean your house. You may need someone to bring you food. These are the things you need right now.

Make sure you have a variety of consistent, weekly support, e.g., seeing a therapist, support group meetings, family dinners, and regular bodywork or acupuncture. Your support and engagement with community has to be LOCKED into your routine and consistent. At no time should you ever feel alone, abandoned, or forgotten. I found Sundays to be the hardest days: while most of my friends were busy carrying on with their regularly scheduled lives, I was alone on the couch, crying for hours, with nothing to do and nowhere to go. You may feel like isolating yourself and not leaving the house or doing anything on Saturdays or Sundays, but I highly recommend that you make sure to have company or stay a little busy. Try to do something on the weekends, and not just spend them by yourself.

RESIST SUICIDAL URGES

You're in an incredibly fragile and vulnerable state during the shock and despair stage. Feeling suicidal yourself is a normal part of this stage. Of course you are considering suicide. Someone close to you crossed the inherent taboo line that we as humans have around suicide. He/she *actually* did kill themself. They bridged that chasm, and in doing so they've made suicide seem like a possible exit strategy for you and your pain, as well as a magical solution to the problem of missing your loved one.

Once a person commits suicide, that act tends to give others permission to kill themselves too. When another acts on this impulse, this is what is known as a "copycat suicide." There are more suicides out there than homicides. However, because of the copycat nature of suicide, the media, historically, hasn't reported them as much as they report homicide.

Because of the immediacy of your beloved's suicide, your despair and longing to be with them, the permissive nature of suicides, and the sort of magical, otherworldly spell that you're under in these early stages of grief, you are at risk for your own suicide. You may be feeling the longing to join your partner in death. I urge you not to. Think of the pain and suffering your beloved's death has caused you. This is what your suicide will inflict on your friends and family for generations. Suicide is a black scar of trauma that hurts not just your immediate friends and family but also siblings and children of those close to the survivor. Do not underestimate how long-lasting and excruciating the impact of suicide is on survivors.

If you are feeling suicidal, the first step is to recognize this as a symptom of being a survivor of suicide. It's a direct result. Tell yourself that it's a symptom of your trauma and not a real solution to your pain. Reach out to loved ones or professionals immediately. The suicide hotline 1-800-SUICIDE is a good starting point for those dark moments.

SEEK THERAPY

You also need a therapist. I highly recommend a trauma specialist or a grief specialist, or both. You need someone who has training and experience in grief, suicide, or trauma and who can simply listen and allow you to grieve, as well as help mitigate your PTSD symptoms. Make sure you find someone who is a good fit for you. Therapy is only effective if you like your therapist and feel she/he gets you. Most of your early sessions might just be you crying and the therapist holding space for your grief. That's okay. You may need to sit and simply cry in therapy for a year, or even longer. That may not seem like it's having a therapeutic effect, but it is.

Crying in a private session with a skilled and trained grief or trauma specialist is different than crying with a loved one, friend, or family member. Most people around you will not know what to say or do in response to your pain. It may be awkward or hard for them to say or do the right thing, because most people don't know what to say or do when someone dies, let alone when someone has killed himself. They may start talking about things that are off-topic or that are unintentionally unsympathetic.

They may make the conversation about themselves and relate it to their divorce or breakup or the death of their mother. While they may mean well, this kind of comparison is absolutely invalidating to your experience and could have a negative effect, making you feel unseen, dismissed, or angry. A good therapist has the background, training, and sophistication to know what to say and what not to say and when, to support your grief, and to facilitate the process along with intention. Even if you're simply going in and crying each session, you're receiving benefits, though you may not feel that at first.

The therapy hour acts as a container for your pain; it focuses solely on you, acknowledging your loss and your beloved. The focus in your sessions should always be on you, never on your therapist. Consistent weekly therapy has a cumulative effect and provides you with a specially designated time to go deeper and deeper with your feelings. Over time, this professionally guided deepening will allow you to move through the grieving process with awareness, empathy, support, and the tools you need in order to rebuild your life.

SIGNS OF TRAUMA, DISSOCIATION, AND SHOCK AND WHAT TO DO ABOUT THEM

Shock is a normal response to death and grief. It is the first stage of grief and an immediate effect of having suffered a trauma. The other stages are bargaining, depression, anger, and finally acceptance. You can go through all these stages at any time and in any sequence. You might feel all of them in one day, or multiple times a day. You may feel clusters of these emotions all at the same time. For example, you may feel depression and anger at the same time. You may be bargaining and sad at the same time while still feeling shock. This is completely normal, and yet also all-consuming and exhausting. So be aware that you are feeling these feelings and that they are completely normal, and that you will feel tired.

Also, everyone grieves differently, and there is no right way or wrong way to go through your grief. The important thing is that you actually grieve—that you allow yourself to feel the pain and go through the stages. If you don't do the hard work of grieving, the grief will get stuck in your nervous system and in your subconscious and eventually start to bleed out into your life and your behaviors at a later time. This is what psychologists call "unresolved" or "complicated" grief. What you don't handle now, you will feel the effects of later. Unfortunately.

I'm writing this almost ten years after John's suicide, and I still think about him and miss him. I still cry and feel the pain of his death and how it's scarred me. Most of the time I'm fine, and I don't think about it. But every once in a while, when I'm processing something, I hit a new layer of grief related to his death. These are subtle and nuanced layers of grief, not the big waves of the first few years, but they are still deeply painful. And all I can do is give myself permission to surrender to them.

shock

Shock is a fuzzy, dissociated feeling. Everything is a bit dreamy or surreal. Dissociation is feeling like you're floating outside your body and can't feel yourself within your skin. People often dissociate after a trauma because the pain of what is happening to them is unbearable and hard to feel. So we pop out of our bodies, so to speak, in order to cope and survive. This is an immediate, short-term reaction. However, it is not a viable or healthy way to live long-term. The best way to help yourself "get back in your body" and stop dissociating is to work with a therapist who specializes in trauma and learn how to reconnect to yourself.

Allow yourself time to be in shock. Shock is one of the stages of grief that is most intangible; people don't realize they're in shock while they're in shock. You may find yourself saying things like: "I can't believe this is happening"; "I don't know why this is happening"; "I don't know what's happening"; and "What's going on?" You may feel really confused, spacey, or exhausted. This is shock.

Grief is exhausting. This kind of traumatic event is going to take a long time for your mind and nervous system to process and understand. Suicide is not a normal, everyday, or natural event. It's not meant to happen. It goes against what we believe is normal or natural. Suicide is a terrifying form of death. Death—especially self-inflicted death—is not something that we as a society have normalized. Your mind simply cannot comprehend that this happened.

Know that that is happening, and that it will be a long time—maybe months, maybe years—before you'll be able to accept that this happened. Until you've reached the stage of acceptance, keep using the guidelines in this book to grieve fully, and do your best to also incorporate some transformational tools into your daily life. Know that this is a process and that it will take the time that it takes. It's impossible to know exactly how long that will be for you. As best as you can, and I know this can be a tall order, try to hold on and have faith that things will get better in time.

If you're experiencing PTSD, you may be:

- Reliving the scene of your beloved's death.
- Experiencing confusion and disorientation.
- Startling easily.
- Experiencing nightmares or flashbacks.
- Avoiding thoughts about the death.
- Having sleep challenges.

- Existing in a state of hypervigilance—always feeling like you're on guard, especially around stimuli that remind you of your beloved's mode of suicide. (I was hypervigilant about trains for years.)
- And possibly also experiencing many other symptoms. It's best to see a professional for help.

how to treat PTSD, shock, and dissociation

Ideally, you will work with someone who can help you learn to "resource" yourself, meaning teach you the skills you need to calm yourself down and regulate your emotions when you feel flooded by feelings or overcome with grief. Resourcing usually entails breathing exercises, grounding exercises, and visualization techniques. Once you have learned these skills, the therapist will use specific techniques to help release the trauma from your nervous system. EMDR therapy and Somatic Experiencing are the two types of trauma therapy I recommend.

Other ways to help with shock and dissociation are grounding techniques and anything somatic or body-related. Examples of some grounding solutions include:

- Eating root vegetables, such as sweet potatoes and squashes.
- Spending time in nature.
- "Earthing"—a technique where you put your bare feet on the earth for at least thirty minutes per day. Putting your feet in sand or saltwater/ocean water is also grounding.
- Getting bodywork, such as fascia-release work, therapeutic massage, or acupuncture. This brings you into greater awareness of what it feels like to be in your skin and will help soothe your nervous system.

WHY ARE WE SO AFRAID TO CRY?

"They" say "the only way out is through." And it's fucking annoying and cliché. But it's true. This grieving is a crazy journey. Madness. Insanity. Never-ending, in some ways. But it is also transformative, if you allow it and shape it. Your shell's been cracked open and something new is emerging. If you go in there and live it, experience it like your life depends on it (and it does), I guarantee that when you pop out the other side of it, you will be different. You will feel things in new ways and experience life from a perspective you never thought possible. You might not want to hear it, you might not see it or believe it, and you certainly don't want it, but I invite you to feel it as fully as you can. Your power is in there. Claim it. Get what's yours.

In various areas of my life, and in my work especially, I hear people commenting, "I got too emotional, so I stopped myself from crying," or "I can't read that—it makes me cry," or "I just don't want to go down that rabbit hole." I've had clients tell me they just can't let themselves cry or grieve, that crying is a sign of weakness and they need to be strong, hold it together. "Dad never allowed crying in his house." I hear this a lot. This fear of crying is like an epidemic in our culture.

I can understand it, of course. Before John passed, I found the idea of showing emotion—real emotion—in public mortifying. And it would have been abominable for me to actually shed tears in front of anyone. That was something I kept to myself. I only allowed myself to cry in the privacy of my room, behind closed doors.

All that changed, with or without my consent, when John killed himself. During that time, I found myself breaking into tears on the phone with friends as I shared word that he was lying unconscious in the hospital, possibly on his deathbed, sobs, sounds I never heard myself make, flew out of me. I tried to speak, but words couldn't come out. From then on, the tears flowed and flowed and didn't stop. I would be grocery shopping at Trader Joe's, hear a love song that reminded me of him, and begin to sob uncontrollably and have to leave the store. I cried in the car, driving up and down through the streets, the cemetery of the world I used to know with John. I cried in class, on my front porch, on my back porch. Everywhere. I cried at the beach, at the edge of the bay, in the woods, at the movies, on the kitchen floor. My tears expressed everything, every feeling I couldn't possibly name and then some—sadness, loss, despair, rage, anguish, longing, isolation, separation, alienation, death, love, hope, beauty, futility, apathy. All of life, the totality of the human experience, is awash in these tears, which I continue to cry to this day.

I know it's painful, I know it's hard to feel so much at times; we feel like we will lose our minds, lose ourselves to the tears, be swallowed up into the depths of the ocean and never find our way back. But why would we deny ourselves this experience? This is the stuff of life. This is why we came here. To fully feel it all. Why would we bypass this part and attempt to only feel joy and light? I do know the value of feeling joy in every moment (this is one of the curious byproducts of an intensive grieving process . . . go figure); however, skipping over the darkness and the pain to get to the light and the transcendent and the spiritual does not lead to wholeness or complete healing. The journey is to integrate the dark with the light, the pain with the pleasure, the human with the divine/transcendent, until they ultimately become one and the same. So you can walk in the dark and *be* the illumination and not feel threatened or scared, knowing that you will not become corrupted or lose yourself.

When I let myself feel it all and cry, the tough emotions—the sadness, anguish, despair, even my longing to die—eventually it gets dried up for a time. My heart opens and what needed to be cleansed moves through and gets released.

The more we cry, the more we heal. So why not cry your heart out and let yourself heal as fully as you can? That's what our tears are for. There's so much excruciating pain in this world, and it is beautiful. The imperfection of it all; our capacity to feel loss and sorrow in addition to joy and happiness; this is what connects us to our humanity—our multifaceted, mixed bag of strengths and flaws, our powerlessness, and the uniquely spiritual quality of own personal narrative of life. The Japanese call it *wabi sabi*. Your heart has been broken and lies in pieces. There's no going back. Embrace the beauty of its brokenness by crying your heart out.

TAKEAWAYS

- Take care of your basic needs: eating, sleeping, exercising as best as possible.
- Get a good therapist as soon as possible.
- Acknowledge that you're in shock. Understand that you've been traumatized.
- Be with the despair, allow it, acknowledge it, and cry.
- If you're feeling suicidal, reach out to others immediately. Call 1-800-SUICIDE if you need someone to talk to. I used to work at this hotline in Los Angeles. The staff are amazing human beings.
- Remember your loved one who passed and share your memories of them with friends and family.
- Don't isolate. Be in community.
- Let yourself be held. Don't underestimate the healing that comes from touch.

shifting

This section explores the process by which I began to be proactive about getting out of my pain and suffering. I started practices that changed my awareness of life, death, and myself. As I changed my perspective and identity, my consciousness began to shift and evolve. It's an ongoing process that continues to this day, even ten years after John's death. I expect it will continue for the rest of my life as I keep growing and cultivating my relationship to life and to death.

FROM: MAIL DELIVERY SUBSYSTEM MAILER-DAEMON@ GOOGLEMAIL.COM

TO: SARAH***@GMAIL.COM

DATE: SUN, AUG 16, 2009 AT 1:31 PM

SUBJECT: DELIVERY STATUS NOTIFICATION (FAILURE)

....

This is an automatically generated Delivery Status Notification

Delivery to the following recipient failed permanently:

john***********@yahoo.com

Technical details of permanent failure:
Google tried to deliver your message, but it was rejected by the recipient domain. We recommend contacting the other email provider for further information about the cause of this error. The error that the other server returned was: 554 554 delivery error: dd. Sorry your message to john***********@yahoo.com cannot be delivered. This account has been disabled or discontinued [#102]. - mta175.mail.sp2.yahoo.com (state 18).

··

Fuck. I'm outside a coffee shop in San Francisco. I tried sending you my last chapter, but the email was returned with the message: "account disabled or discontinued." The trees across the street began to slant; the sky is spinning. I'm spinning out again. Reality cracking again. Has your mom or brother been accessing your account and seen my emails? Did they shut down your account? I don't want to bother them by asking such weird questions. Your email and that part of you is officially gone. Obliterated from the universe. I already knew you were gone, but this feels like another mini death. I didn't know where to send the rest of my emails, so I created a new email address for you so I can continue to send you these letters. The username is similar to your old one. Wherever you are, I'm sure you'll get these emails, whether you check the account or not.

Love,
Sarah

Dear John,

I was hurt when you avoided my question about living together. All I wanted was to spend more time with you. I know making rent was hard: you had a sweet deal living at Barbara and Jean's and you couldn't afford anything more than $300 a month. I know you were scared of taking a new step in commitment to our relationship. I used to fantasize about a sweet little home life with you: unwinding on the couch with a glass of wine; dancing in the kitchen together as we prepared something yummy, like that cinnamon-infused lamb tagine we used to make; sitting at the table doing our work together while stealing glances over our laptops, hugging during our breaks, and taking quick walks around the block for energy and motivation; curling up in bed and watching a movie while falling asleep on your warm chest; waking up to your delicious smell and kind, smiling eyes; starting the day with our morning meditation walk around the neighborhood, then having tea, breakfast, and a shower; and off to school or work and following whatever simple adventures the day might bring. That's all I wanted, day in and day out . . . with you. I waited for it, futilely.

I wished you hadn't used your spiritual practices of "staying in the present moment" and "not projecting a future as a means to avoid the Now" to evade relating, real intimacy, and commitment to a long-term future with me. It was as if you were trying to avoid having any future at all.

You didn't have much experience in relationships, and this tended to make me the teacher in ours. Most of your relating revolved around your spiritual worldview and the maze of confusion it created for you. You used your "spiritual inquiry" on everything you thought or everything anyone else did, to the point where nothing became real, nothing was true, and you were essentially erasing yourself. I wish you wouldn't have fucking spiritually bypassed living a rich, juicy, messy, colorful, paradoxical, human experience with me. You used your transpersonal/spiritual beliefs that the "personal self," the "little me," the egoic and mind-identified self was less than and not as valid as the bigger, more transcended Self (with a capital "s") as your reason for not asking me personal questions and engaging me in conversation (carefree or otherwise) about my inner and outer experiences. When we conversed, it was *me* engaging *you*, and then we spent time talking about you and your processes, and not about me. I hate to say it, but I did get bored at times.

I wanted you to show passion for me and take a real interest in my world. Did you see me? Did you get me? I often wondered. Like the time you visited me in New York and spent most of the trip glued to your computer or with your nose stuck in a journal article, stressing over the upcoming deadline of our dissertation proposal. It was your first time in New York, and it seemed like you couldn't have cared less what we did. I look back and can't believe I led you by the arm through the hot, noisy subway as you walked and read a research article. You were pretty detached from the city and you didn't even look up once to see any of the spectacle of life occurring all around you. You didn't make much effort, not even for my sake. It was like your body was in New York but your mind was somewhere else, overwhelmed with fear. I wanted to alleviate your anxiety; I tried to help. That's why I navigated you through the subway, to give you a bit more time to get your work done and to give you incentive to get out and have dinner at one of my favorite Italian restaurants in the East Village. It was like I had to bribe you with the assurance that you could get reading done on the train just to get you to participate in sharing my city with you. And even after all that, you didn't think the restaurant was that special.

I felt insecure and doubted that you were *into* me at all (oh, that stupid question!). I wanted earthly, passionate, sublime love. You wanted a relationship that would facilitate your spiritual growth. I often felt used, perhaps like your prom date, and got pissed at you for this. Over the course of our relationship, my mind festered with doubts. I struggled to figure out if we were right for each other. Were we a match? The love was there; it was warm, yummy, and palpable. I just had to look in your kind, innocent eyes and I melted, every time. And yet . . .

In order to alleviate my doubts, I proceeded to dump them and my insecurities on you. I pointed out your shortcomings and insisted that you try to become the man I wanted you to be, the man I believed would be my perfect match. I know this cut you up inside like a sharp, broken CD and infected you with insecurities of your own. It made you feel you were a burden on me. John, I'm sorry I did this to you. On top of everything else you were dealing with, you certainly didn't need my insecurities and my overly critical mental analysis. I hope you've forgiven me. You tried hard to address my concerns and improve yourself to meet my crazy standards. I cringe as I look back and see what a bitch I was at times. It pains me. And it's the truth. I wish I could have been as sweet as you. I hope I'm a kinder person now. I've had time to reflect and learn from the best.

If only we could have fully shut off the noise in our heads. I wish I had lived from my heart and savored each moment with you instead of questioning it. I wish we both hadn't let our confused minds get in the way of loving each other. I would never, ever, take a single second with you for granted again. I will never take pure love for granted again. Why do we let our minds take over like this? John, how can I let my heart and body lead the way? I know you'll send me the answers in time.

Yours,
Sarah

....

One crisp, bright, blue-sky morning in late September, I opened my email and saw something from you. My heart jumped, infused with energy. It was a good day!

> *Sarah,*
>
> *I am ready for a hello over here. I am open to tea at Dana St., bike ride around some blocks on your side of the tracks (my preference for now), Sunday afternoon at the farmer's market, and possibly other ideas that you might have. I am free for the tea, bike ride, or something you have in mind tonight between 5p and 7p, anytime Sunday, and Monday morning before class. I may end up seeing you at Ashley's party but I was also invited to Mokie's party in Santa Cruz before I found out about Ashley's party last night (yahoo or I lost my evite). I never know anymore what I am doing Saturdays. It's all about what it feels like that day. I think I have heard that said somewhere before. :) Well, time for practicum.*
>
> *Happy Friday,*
> *John*
>
> *PS Thanks for letting me know about your request for less gooshy sweetness. I can't promise that I won't slip up everyone once in a while, but am trying my best.*

What a cute email you wrote. I wasn't quite sure if this would be good for me. After all, I was acutely aware of how deeply you had broken my heart when you said that you were never in love with me and couldn't see yourself in love with me. Your flip-flopping confusion had hurt me terribly, especially after you'd volunteered to convert to Judaism so early in our relationship in order to make my family happy. I wasn't sure what we would be talking about, and I didn't quite trust you. I figured you were dating and playing the field like you'd said you wanted.

Regardless of my mixed feelings, I had to see you, immediately. We made plans to meet for tea at Dana St. Coffee shop later that evening. I made sure, though, that I had plans for later: watching the Obama-McCain presidential debate at Vera's house.

After a long day of leading groups and seeing clients, I rushed to the gym, rushed home, showered, and put on jeans and lay-ered two different-colored tank tops, trying to look casually sexy. I had cut my hair shorter— a little above my shoulders. You hadn't seen this look yet and I wondered what you'd think. When I arrived at Dana St., I spotted you through the window. I trembled with nervousness and excitement; I tried to keep my arms and legs moving in a normal fashion so they wouldn't give away the fact that I was shaking. We said hello politely. I did not want to get a hug from you or touch you and feel your warm body. That would be my downfall. You broke up with *me*, I had to keep reminding myself.

We sat at a square table and talked over steaming cups of tea. You looked tired and not as handsome as I remembered. A cold sore cut across your lip. I felt triumphant; I looked better than you. As if it was a competition to see who was faring better. In some ways it was, for me. I shared the stages of grief I'd been cycling through—the denial, the anger, the depression, and the acceptance—for the past month and a half. You listened and gave me that old, mesmerized look with your wide eyes. I felt oddly uncomfortable that you appeared in awe, still so innocent. What was I doing here? I wasn't sure.

"I've been struggling." You looked at me, your eyes flecked with yellow. "I've missed you, Sarah."

I wanted to tell you the same, how *much* I missed you, but I just couldn't. It wasn't fair to me. I wasn't going to let you get off the hook that easily.

"You need to know how deeply you broke my heart. And I'm not sure you know that," I said. My intention was not to make you feel guilty but to inform you of the facts.

Forehead lined, eyes squinted, you let out a sigh. "I'm sorry, Sarah . . . I realized . . . that . . . that many times in our discussions—I was not there for you. This little, scared boy showed up, and I got caught up with him . . ." Your voice trailed off and you looked at your hands. "I wasn't able to see past my scared little boy fears and be available to you over there." You looked me straight in the eye, pleading. "I am deeply sorry for that."

I averted my gaze, I couldn't get trapped in your eyes again. "Wow. That's a really big insight, John. I'm impressed you were able to realize that. Thank you."

"I also know I attached to believing . . . you were able to control me, and the payoff for that—was . . . I didn't have to take responsibility for my choice to be with you in case things didn't work out and people got hurt. I did choose to be with you Sarah—emotionally, physically, mentally, and spiritually.

And things haven't worked out and people are hurt . . . and I'm responsible . . . I deeply apologize for the times I was unwilling to take responsibility for my choice to be in our relationship."

I exhaled. "I have waited a long time to hear you say that. I think that's more fair to both of us. Thank you for taking responsibility. I needed to hear that."

We talked carefully, about this and that. You were still finding a topic for your dissertation. You'd had a couple of ideas but had thrown them out the window. You had recently met with Byron Katie and were thinking of doing your research on the psychospiritual effects of her spiritual inquiry process. I was secretly concerned about your not having a topic as of yet; we were about to start the dissertation class, and our topics needed to be finalized and researched by this point in the year. I held myself back from giving you any help, and supported whatever you thought you wanted to do. The important thing, I said, was to keep moving along with it. I told you about my new presence practices, how I listened to Tolle all the time and went to various satsangs and meditated often.

You told me you hadn't been dating other women. I found that a relief. You said you wanted to be friends. I said I didn't know if that was possible. Many people, and especially my mom, had been cautioning me against being friends with you. They thought if we stayed friends, I'd never get over you. I think they were right.

John, it felt easy to fall back into our space and fall back into the lightness of your blue eyes. I knew that for my own sanity, I had to go, had to get out of your vicinity. It was time to go watch the presidential debate.

You walked me to my car and the rhythm of our talking and walking felt right. Our energies seemed to naturally merge with one another, like old times, and that enveloped us in our bubble once again. Back in our own world, it was hard to say goodbye and leave you. The love between us was still there. Nothing could turn it off. But what would happen between us was unknown.

You were growing and becoming more of a man. Would you develop a warrior-like side and pursue me? Could I be fulfilled by you? Could the walls I'd put up against you in the last month and a half since our breakup come down? Could I trust you?

I was still sleeping when I heard knocking on my back door. I rolled over and saw that it was 9:00 a.m. I opened the door gingerly, wearing my white pajamas. You stood in the doorway holding a bouquet of red roses, the same bouquet as the last time you brought flowers. Your face looked sheepish, but somewhat relieved. "Sarah, I've made a huge mistake," you said.

I was too sleepy to feel excited. I was surprisingly level-headed. I'd played out this scenario in my head many times, but never imagined it in my pajamas with bed-head. "Okay. Um, give me a minute. Why don't you have a seat in the living room? I'll just be a minute."

I went to the bathroom, brushed my teeth, and straightened up. I sat down opposite you. Your eyes had shadows underneath them. You looked scared.

"What's going on, John?"

"Sarah. Oh Sarah. I've made a huge mistake. Can you please forgive me?"

"What are you talking about?"

"I *am* in love with you. I realized I've been in love with you ever since you wrote that poem about me in journaling class. I just didn't know it. I don't want to be without you anymore. I want to spend the rest of my life with you."

"I'm not sure about this. I thought you wanted to be with other women?"

"I don't. I can't . . . I couldn't do it. No one else could compare to you. I couldn't look at other women. All I saw was you everywhere. No one else compares to your beauty. I drove by your house some nights just to try and see you."

I was speechless. I sat for a while, not knowing what to say.

"Sarah, sweet Sarah. I'm sorry," you said. "Please have me back."

"I don't know what to say, John. I don't understand. You said you weren't in love with me and that you never could be. But now you're here."

"I know. I'm so sorry. I thought that was my truth, I really did. And now . . . I know that was me not wanting to subject you to me anymore. I thought you deserved to be with someone better."

"Can you let me make that decision for myself?"

"I know I hurt you. Please let me make it up to you. If you'll have me."

"I don't know if I can trust you again. I have too many walls up now."

"Whatever I can do . . . to go slowly with you . . . we can go as slowly as you need."

I sat, pondering and watching you.

"Can I come sit next to you?" you asked meekly.

I nodded. You came over. I turned to you, your large eyes looked pained. You were so close, I could feel the heat coming off your body.

"John, things would have to be different this time around."

"Yes," you said. "Can I hold your hand, Sarah?"

I smiled weakly. I could feel my walls melting already. This was you. *You.* And I had a hard time resisting. You gently reached for my hand, and as our hands touched, I sighed inside.

I knew many women—my mom and a few girlfriends—would tell me to resist you, to hold out for longer and test you, make you work for it. But I couldn't. I was so happy you'd come back. I wanted the immediate gratification of being with you again.

We sat together for a long time, staring at each other without speaking. You were lost without me, you said. I knew the feeling. Even though I was doing well, my life didn't make sense without you in it.

You asked if you could kiss me. I said yes (how could I not?) and surrendered a part of myself to you, but not all of me just yet. The kiss was dangerous, like doing something I knew I shouldn't. I did it anyway.

In the late-morning sun, we walked arm in arm through the farmers market, shopping for white peaches and heirloom tomatoes. We spoke of trips we would take to San Diego and a cruise vacation you'd won somewhere. Things would have to be different. I made sure you knew this. I told you I wouldn't be meeting you all the way anymore. You had to show up and meet me halfway. You had to take responsibility in the relationship. During our breakup, I'd learned more about our dynamic, about myself, and about my tendencies in relationships, how much I had extended myself and given to be with you, to be the lucky girl worthy of being your girlfriend. Once I'd seen the situation clearly, there was no going back.

Something felt different about you, like you were flattened and stale—perhaps even more confused than before—but I couldn't put my finger on it.

That evening, we worked on our dissertations. I dove into work, but you couldn't. You said you were having anxiety and asked if we could take a minute to "check in" and see how we were doing, emotionally speaking. I plopped down next to you on the couch.

"What's going on?" I asked.

"I'm noticing I'm having some panic come up—about not being able to do this?"

"Not being able to do what?"

"Be in relationship with you and get my schoolwork done at the same time."

I took a deep breath. "John, at this point, you don't really have a choice, do you? I mean you've tried to not be with me and that didn't work out. So that's not an option. And you have to get your schoolwork done, so there's no choice there either. We'll just do it one step at a time."

Your eyes widened, as if you understood and accepted what I said. "You're right, Sarah. You're so good. You're so good."

"I know you can do this, John. You can."

We sat down and did a few hours of work. But still I felt like something was off; you weren't acting like yourself, you weren't quite all there. After eating a simple dinner, we went to sleep, sharing the same bed for the first time in a while. I treasured this.

In the morning, I rolled over and gazed at your sweet face. You wrapped your arms around me.

"Morning. How'd you sleep?" I asked.

"Um, not so well. I didn't."

"You didn't sleep? How come?"

"I was up thinking." You paused and took a deep breath. "I don't know if I can do this again, Sarah. It feels too hard. I feel trapped in obligations and commitment. I'm not sure I'm in love with you."

I rolled away, but you held me against you.

"I don't know what to say anymore, John. This sounds like a bigger problem than being about me. What changed since yesterday?"

"I don't know what's going on. I know I love you. You are amazing. But the fear of measuring up to what you want from me, meeting you halfway . . . I don't know if I can do it. I'm afraid of failing. I'm scared I will be a failure in this relationship and scared of doing this to you again. I'm scared of being a deadbeat like my dad."

"I just don't know what to say anymore, John."

I didn't have time for another long conversation about this. It was the first day of fall classes, and I needed to renew my car registration at the DMV. I needed to get going and start my day. I got up and got dressed.

Could we talk about this later? I asked before I left the house. At my car, I realized I'd forgotten my keys. Back in the house, I called to you. You were sitting on my bed, staring off into space. You turned to me, your eyes filled with such sorrow. My heart wrenched with sadness. I recognized the look on your face. I've worn it before, sitting and clutching my head after my own suicide attempt.

"John? Are you okay?"

"I don't know. I don't know anything anymore."

I took your hand. I know how it feels when the earth opens up and the room starts to spin. I was not going to leave you alone with your head during a nervous breakdown.

"Do you want to come with me to the DMV? I don't want to leave you alone right now. Why don't you come with me?"

You nodded, consenting like a child.

"It's gonna be okay, John. I promise you, everything will be okay."

You broke into sobs. "Oh god. Oh god, Sarah. I don't know what's wrong with me. I can't keep doing this to you. I can't. You have such a bright future ahead of you. I see it all for you. You're going to go so far and do such good work. I can't do that. There's no future for me. I don't want to end up in the hospital."

"John, don't say that. You're not going to end up in the hospital. John. You are such a good therapist. You are so talented with teenagers. Your clients love you. And any work that I do professionally, you're going to be right there with me. Together. We're going to work together. If we succeed, we succeed together. If we fail, we fail together. It will be okay."

At this point, we were in my car. I had not let go of your hand. I held tight, hoping to keep you grounded, keep you from unraveling entirely.

"I don't want to get institutionalized."

"No one is going to institutionalize you. I promise you. I promise you."

Your body shook with tears. You let out a wail. You tried to speak but sobs choked your words. Pain gushed from a place within you I had never seen.

"I can't keep doing this to you. You don't deserve this. I'm so ashamed." You covered your face with your hands. "Everyone in your life must hate me for this."

"No, they don't, John. You know our friends love you."

Your sobs got louder.

"I wish I could be in love with you. Oh god. I can't keep doing this to you. I wish I knew why this is happening to me. Oh god. Oh god." You twisted in your seat. "I'm worthless. Oh god . . ."

"Listen to me, John. I'm here. I love you. You are not worthless. We need to get you some help. Can you see a therapist? Or Dr. Lee?"

"I have no money. Oh god . . . I lost my money . . . the bank collapse . . . lost everything I saved."

I held your hand tightly. You cried at the DMV. People noticed as I led you by the hand. While I spoke with the designated agent, you slumped against the counter and hung your head in your arms. I was petrified for you but kept a poker face.

Outside, in the crowded parking lot, I asked you to stick the orange September registration sticker on my license plate. I hoped this might orient you back to the world. You placed it with care on top of red 2007.

"Yay!" I clapped like a proud mommy. "I finally have my registration sticker!"

Through tears, you smiled feebly. That sticker is still there, underneath blue 2009.

"Let's go for breakfast. I think we deserve some pancakes and milkshakes."

I took you to Denny's, thinking that a pancake breakfast would comfort you, that eating might help you feel grounded. We sat in a booth in the back. Ants scurried along the edge of the table like bandits, knowing full well they shouldn't be there. I found their presence repulsive. I looked at them. I looked at you.

"Do you want to move?" I asked.

"I want to do whatever you want to do. It feels better to be next to you," you said. "I want to be wherever you are, Sarah."

We switched tables and I hugged you. Sometimes pancakes and milkshakes can help you forget your troubles. Sometimes they can't.

You continued to cry in the car on the drive to school. We had separate classes and I couldn't keep an eye on you. You wore yesterday's clothes. You didn't look well. Regardless of whether you and I got back together, regardless of your feelings for me, I needed to be there for you. It was that simple.

After class, I took your hand. We drove to my place. You were about to ride home on your bike.

"Thank you, Sarah." You stared at me through swollen, red eyes. In that instant, your mind went static again. Sobs poured from your throat. You, the most athletically coordinated and gifted person I knew, couldn't get on your bike and ride home.

My heart broke. I wished I knew what was happening, why you were in uncontrollable pain. I didn't understand. Your explanations didn't sufficiently explain the amount or depth of the pain and tears moving through you. Most of your answers were muffled through sobs. I tried to follow along, but your speech was confusing. My heart beat rapidly, my chest constricted, and my ribs ached. I was simply there, offering what empathy and support I could. I wished I could help you and take away that otherworldly pain. I gathered you to me and walked you to the bedroom to lie down and rest.

I rested my head on your chest and held you tightly. Your tears turned to cries of needle-piercing pain.

"Why can't I be in love with you? What is wrong with me? I don't deserve this. I don't deserve you. Any other man . . . would be lucky to have you just for a day. Why? Ohhhhhh. Ahhh. Why can't I just be in love with you and give you everything you deserve? Oh. My god."

More grief thundered through you, with such momentum that you couldn't have stopped it even if you'd tried. Its force even rippled through me. I was helpless and had never felt this utter sense of sadness for anyone or anything before. I cried into your sweat-soaked shirt and held on tightly.

The sun was setting and the room gradually filled with darkness. I tried to distract you from the onslaught of pain by doing "therapy" with you: talking with the scared little boy you'd mentioned you'd found. I asked what the little boy was scared of. He was scared of failing, you said, shuddering. I asked if there were other parts of you that could talk to the little boy and help him feel less scared, help him grow up and know that everything is okay when he gets older.

"John, is there maybe a cool, wise, high school quarterback in there?"

Silence for a second. You nodded. Yes, you'd found him.

"I bet he's super sexy and confident. Always knowing where to throw the ball and how to call and run those plays. I bet all the girls at school love him, and he's a great leader on the team. His teammates look up to him and trust him. Could that cool, confident high school quarterback say something to your little boy?"

There was more silence.

"John. What is he saying?"

"He's saying, 'There's nothing to lose.'" Your voice cracked. "There's nothing to ever lose," you repeated louder. "OH GOD. OH GOD," you sobbed.

"John, John, take a deep breath. Come back here for a moment."

I tried to guide you into your present moment awareness by reminding you of Eckhart Tolle. You quieted for a few minutes. But soon your wailing began again.

I held you for three hours as your body tremored with sobs. *How much longer can I do this?* I wondered. I needed to start my schoolwork. Absorbing your pain wasn't good for me, even though my heart ached for you.

I left the room to call Barbara. I explained the situation and asked for her to pick you up. She was entertaining guests but would come over as soon as they left. I made tea. We sat in the living room. I went over your options for getting therapy. I was clear that you needed to talk to someone. I wasn't sure if I should be that person because of how entangled we were, how mixed my feelings were. I suggested talking to one of your best friends, Brett. He was a few years ahead of us at school and on his way as a therapist. I imagined he'd be good with you and of course wouldn't charge you anything. You never did work with him, though. In hindsight, I should have loaned you money and insisted you use it to see our old therapist in Berkeley. I'm sure she could have helped you. I should have insisted you see our acupuncturist again. God. I wish I'd known to do that.

After Barbara picked you up, I was flooded with tears of my own. I've never beheld anyone in such pain; it was the saddest thing I've ever seen. I was overwhelmed with my own helplessness. I called Sophie and cried about my worries for you. We decided it would be best if I called your best friend, Brandon, told him about the situation, and told him to rally up your closest male friends, have them do their best to support you, counsel you, and check in with you. I hung up and immediately called Brandon. I cried on the phone with him too. He said he would go over to your house and check up on you.

In fucking hindsight, I wish I'd called your mom in Oklahoma that night and told her that something was very wrong and she needed to take care of you. It didn't even occur to me to call her, though. I mean, I guess I figured you were a grown man and eventually everything would be fine.

I changed the soaking wet sheets on my bed; they were covered in sadness. I wasn't sure how to feel or what to do. On the one hand I loved you so fucking much and was bludgeoned with sadness at seeing you this way. I wished, as I always wished, that I could do something to transfer your burden to my shoulders so I could deal with it, shape it, and move through it for you. At the same time I was torn by the need to protect myself from you. How many times would you break my heart? How many times were you going to love me then tell me you weren't in love with me? How much longer could I subject myself to your confusion and then stand there and hold your hand through it? A part of me was angry at you for coming back to me then revoking it the next day. This part of me was overshadowed, however, by my terror for your well-being. Regardless of your chronic confusion about your feelings for me, which probably caused you even more pain and heartache than it caused me, the humane part of me won out: I had to be a friend to you. Of the people in your life, I was closest to you and knew you best (Brandon and Ben knew you as deeply, but in different ways). I was also the one who knew firsthand about the extent of this inexplicable pain and was best equipped to help you through this dark time. I felt I needed to be there for you and try hard to not get sucked into your pain, your confusion.

Brandon texted me: he'd gone over to your house, you seemed fine, everything was okay. I didn't quite believe that was possible, but accepted his word and went to bed. I prayed for something better to reveal itself in the morning.

If only I could have erased your suffering.

With regret,
Sarah

My supervisor at my practicum site reminded me often that I hadn't been your therapist. You had a therapist, and as your girlfriend, it wasn't my job to play that role. The seeds for what you did were planted a long time ago, before I even knew you, she'd said. Your problems were rooted more deeply than anyone had known. This resonated for me, and hearing it shifted something inside: I experienced my own frailty, my humanity. I had so wanted to save you and rescue you from your confusion and pain. What I want to say to you now (and I'm sure you know this already, but it's worth repeating in writing, at least for me)—is that you are the one who is 100 percent responsible for what you did and for what happened. No one else. I am not responsible. You are. God knows I've felt responsible and blamed myself for not having superhuman powers to redeem your fate, to have foreseen your death, and to swoosh in and scoop you up off the train tracks in the nick of time. It's been a sobering lesson internalizing this truth about myself. As much as I wish I did, I don't have that kind of power. I'm only human. And despite my limitations, I felt an irrepressible urge to take care of you as fiercely as I could (God only knows how limited my hands are). At the end of each day, I burn with the question, could we have saved you?

If only,
Sarah

....

Dear John,

Time stood still on November 7th, 2008, the day you died. Days, weeks, and months surely were crossed off calendars around the world, but for me life stopped. My birthday came in March and its arrival disoriented and confused me. I was still in November. I couldn't reconcile the plain truth that time had continued. It still doesn't make sense to me now, even though as I write these words I'm more than a year past your death. In some ways it feels like no time has passed and in other ways it seems like it's been a hundred years and life has dragged on and on.

That winter was an endless night. In *The Year of Magical Thinking*, Didion expresses her desire to bring her husband back. I didn't want to bring you *back,* I wanted to go *to* you. I started meditating every morning and evening. I thought if I meditated enough and did all these different spiritual practices, I could have an "awakening" of consciousness and transcend my sense of reality and be with you. I didn't realize it then but I was idealizing you and my pain, trying to cope with your rejection of me, to cope with your death. I was hoping to have an out-of-body experience where I would see you. I wanted to blast my usual mode of consciousness and enter into a state of no-separation between me here, in a physical body, and you there, without form. If I had a spiritual awakening, my sense of time would drastically alter and linear time as I knew it would cease. And then I could live out the rest of my life in a state of enlightened bliss and not feel the drudgery of the next fifty or sixty years of my life. Having an awakening would make my "filler time" until I reached you move as quickly and easily as possible.

Toward this goal, I sought spiritual guidance. I pursued different spiritual teachings that promised awakening through presence practices, like Eckhart Tolle, Adyashanti, Dipa Ma, etc. You would have loved it. I sat in complete stillness in the bath. I meditated in the morning. I meditated in the evening. I kept a dream journal and diligently tried to understand the encrypted messages behind the symbols of my psyche. I sought therapy from two different psychologists: one was Jungian and helped me specifically with dreams; the other was a transpersonalist who sat with me as I cried and cried through each session.

I went to acupuncture. I worked with a shaman who recommended I do a variety of rituals. I brought flowers to the ocean. I made daily offerings to you and the "ancestors" on my meditation altar of wine, ash, honey, cinnamon ('cause you love it), and flowers. I danced my tears out at 5 Rhythms. All this was part of my strategy to reach you, and I was relentless. But it hasn't worked. You're still over there, dead. And I'm still here. Time is the same as ever.

In the spring, I started riding horses. I felt closer to you on a horse because of your cowboy past and your special connection with horses. I imagined that if I galloped fast enough, the horse would lift off and take me to you. In my first lesson, the instructor taught me about the correct posture for riding. "Shoulders back. Gaze out toward the horizon," she said. With my slumped shoulders and cast-down eyes, this was my hardest practice.

Dedicated as I was, even with all my intense seeking and therapy, nothing eased my pain. I grieved hard. I couldn't help but grieve; it was the only thing to do—my tears kept coming. While others were out living their lives or snuggling with loved ones on cold winter nights, I writhed in pain, alone, missing you for hours with no relief. There was nothing that could be done, so I let myself be in pain. Many nights I was too weak to stand up and look in my refrigerator for food. My body slumped to the floor. I lay on the cold linoleum, stomach clenched, tears surrounding me. On other nights I flew into rages, throwing dishes against the kitchen wall. When there was nothing left to throw I lay down on the shards of glass, not caring if I got cut. I missed you so fucking much. Do you GET THAT? I lived on a jagged edge between life and death. I wanted off this edge, either relief through death or a return to an aliveness of the living.

Your Tigerlily

People often asked me if I was angry at you. They were angry at you for me. I know they tried their best to hide it out of respect for me. I don't blame them. I think if I were in their shoes, I'd be angry on their behalf. *How could he do this to her?* I imagined them saying amongst themselves.

And yes, I did ask that question. How could you do this to me? Wasn't I enough of a reason for you to stay? If you really loved me, you would've stayed. How could you be so selfish? I never thought I'd be in this situation. I did not sign up for this. How is this my life? What am I going to do with my life now?

My mind was racked with questions, day and night, trying to make sense of a warped reality that makes no sense. But was I angry at you? Yes, but also no. Since I understand this longing to die, to return home, and since I have gone through many hard struggles with depression and lived most of my life in the dark, I understood what you'd gone through. I understand the constricted mind state, the tunnel vision that someone who wants to kill himself experiences. It's truly black and numb. You can't fathom that anyone else would care if you were gone because you've simply stopped feeling anything that even remotely resembles love. It isn't selfish, like most people think; it's the only self-preserving option a person can fathom in that moment. To kill yourself, to actually do it and die, takes more courage than I can imagine. Our brains and our systems are wired to take every possible precaution against death. So to intentionally counter our biological conditioning is a tremendous feat and speaks to the depths of your pain, suffering, and longing to get out.

For my own sanity, I practiced being happy that you're no longer in pain. It was a relief to know you were in joy and need not suffer another second longer. I had to come to a place where I would prefer your freedom over my need for you to stay on Earth in order to alleviate my pain. I would never want to enslave you in your suffering on my behalf. So my task was to keep digging and healing until I could genuinely accept the choice you'd made and be okay with things as they were, no matter how horrendous everything felt. I was mostly angry at the universe and enraged that this was my life. How could this be my path in life? It was too hard, too lonely, and I resented the challenge. Why was I the only twenty-nine-year-old I knew having to deal with this kind of tragedy while everyone else was happily coupled up or in the process of happily coupling up? There had to be some fucking reason, because to say it fucking sucked is the understatement of the year.

"Sarah, you need to allow yourself to be angry at him," "they" said. And I was like, sure, okay. How do I do that when I'm just not feeling that angry right now? Yes, I was angry at you. I'm not going to pretend I wasn't. My anger at you flared up most often when I was mourning the death of all the dreams I had had for our future. Those were the ones that killed me. I also get angry when I see other people moving along through life "normally" and doing all the conventional, "normal" things like getting married and having kids, on the "normal" timeline of things, and they do it all so easily and effortlessly. And I'm confused. I don't know how they do it. I don't know how to do that for myself. It's like I can't. And I want to, but it seems like an impossibility for me. My scars are too deep. My trauma too unbearable, too unresolvable, though lord knows I try. And that's when I fucking rage. I lose it. It's like I'm trapped in a loop and no matter what I do, I can't get out.

As a psychologist, I understand that anger is a "normal and natural stage of grief." It comes up whether we like it or not, sometimes in the most unexpected ways. But to normalize it like this is to miss the point. This is not your ordinary, run-of-the-mill anger. It's a rage that's summoned from another dimension. It's a possession, really. Thunderbolts and lightning do not do it justice. Feeling my anger, really fucking feeling it and embodying it, was/is essential for my healing, integration, and acceptance. My biggest shifts happened through my rage. It was through my rage, every time, that I grabbed my power, claimed a stake in my own life, and stopped pining for you. I shifted my codependency with you in death. My rage helped me stop feeling suicidal. It gave me myself back. Through my anger, I found more and more strength to go on. It fuels my will to live and actualize in the world.

Bye for now,
Tiger

Dear John,

When you died, my mind was literally blown out in shock. I couldn't comprehend what was happening. And yet a little part of me recognized the truth of what you'd done. Perhaps I had an intuition all along that something like your suicide was brewing, but I wasn't aware of it consciously.

In any case, nothing was more terrifying and painful than the reality that you were gone, forever . . . but at the same time, you also aren't gone. The night that you passed, I had finally fallen asleep with the help of some Ambien, only to wake up sobbing silently in the middle of the night. Reality had become distorted, and waking up to the real nightmare that I would never hold your hand again bolted me into states of internal hysteria. As I lay crying in bed (with my sister Mila asleep next to me), I felt something shift energetically in the room. I felt your presence. The room was warm and light, and I felt peaceful and somewhat relaxed. I knew it was you. And from there we began a conversation. Our dialogue was internal, and I allowed whatever I thought you were saying to come through. Did I hear a voice out loud, speaking crystal-clearly? No. It was an inner speaking in my mind—not of my own usual voice, per se, but using my mind's voice, and it had a distinct feeling to it. Since it was so light and nice, I knew it couldn't be me.

You shared with me that you were now in "splendid joy." That you were deeply sorry for what I was going through but you couldn't continue on as you had been. You and I had decided before we got here to have this experience together—for you to die and for me to survive so that we could work together in this way. It was your job to break my heart open over and over again because it had been locked closed for some time. Well, you succeeded.

I've always had psychic-type abilities, but over the course of my life, whenever I shared my experiences with others, they often thought I was crazy, and in turn I felt weird. So I pushed my abilities aside and buried them. But at age twenty-nine, when you died, my psychic abilities came roaring to the surface again. My hands were literally on fire, hot and sensitive to the touch. For three weeks after you passed it felt like they were burning and the cellular makeup of my body was changing and morphing. Something new was forming.

Ever since that first night, we've been communicating in many ways, and I've been noticing and feeling your presence around me through many things: bluebirds, the twinkling of chimes, my dreams, rainbows, and songs. These signs fill me with comfort and hope. They connect me to a distorted, magical reality different than my grief. These moments of connection with your spirit are still no substitute for you, but at least it's something. At least I can still keep our conversation alive.

To this end, I made it a daily practice to develop my ability to telepathically communicate with you. I sit down every morning and talk to you and receive any feelings or answers I can. The more I practice, the more my abilities blossom.

Since I know you are still alive in some other form, just not in the body I knew, loved, and had been intimate with, I have to reconcile my grief over the loss of your body, the loss of being able to see you with my eyes and touch you with my hands and talk to you in our old way of talking, the loss of thousands of little things. The loss of everything. I have to reconcile all that with this new, emerging awareness of the fact that you didn't completely die; you still live on, just in some other form I cannot recognize with my limited physical senses. This is incredibly hard to do, and still is. It's my practice of having faith. The more signs and confirmations I received from you on the other side, the easier it got. I craved those signs from you. I desperately pleaded for them all the time. They gave me such temporary relief.

No one could really comprehend the unbearable pain and how hard it is to work through it and feel closer to you again. I'll be honest, nothing helps. It just doesn't. But with each day, I move with my pain. I practice with it, and with each step I find a crumb of strength here, a kernel of joy there, and a pearl of wisdom that somehow allows me to take the next step forward.

Always reaching for the sky.

Love,
Sarah

John,

Before you died, I'd been hitting the gym three times a week, dancing, and doing Pilates and yoga. I was in pretty good shape. But after, I could barely feel my body. It was in shock, and I hardly ate, let alone exercise or dance. I didn't have the will to exert any more energy than it took to breathe and get through a day. Two months later, desperate to feel better, I dragged myself back to 5 Rhythms, my dance practice.

At first, I danced slowly, lifelessly, unsure how my body would move in my newfound sense of reality and tragedy. No one in class knew my story or had seen or felt the terror I'd been through. A part of me wanted everyone to know exactly what it took to stand in the middle of a room full of moving bodies and sway my head to the beat. Another part of me relished my anonymity. A particular song came on that you and I used to dance to. I dropped to my knees in child's pose, grateful for my privacy, and cried tears onto the floor. You were there, no doubt, dancing with me.

As the night marched on, I leaned into the company of the beautiful, brave people dancing around me. It was their joy for life, their sorrow, their bare feet pounding on the floor, their endless, adorable movements, their yelps of excitement, and their passion for dance that reminded me of the infinite beauty of humanity. I felt grateful to be a part of this brute display of sweat, prayers, and tears. The dance of life happening all around me, regardless of my trauma. My spirit was gaining strength. When my life felt like it had stopped, the rest of the world kept on dancing and saved a place for me. That night, I realized that no matter what, I, too, could just keep dancing.

When there's nothing left to do, I dance.

With you,
Sarah

....

John,

Our so-called "prom" in June, seven months after your death, put me at an all-time low. The prom was a marker of time passing and our advancement to the next stage of our program, from classes to internship. You should have been there with us, wrapping up classes and working exclusively on our dissertations and internship hours. If only you'd held on a little longer, you could have made it through and would have celebrated the closure of a hard third year. The prom was a sad reminder that as we moved on and pulled through, you hadn't. At orientation, they'd told us to look around the room; one in three people would not graduate the program. They hadn't said the cause would be death.

Dressed in my navy and lace vintage halter dress, I sat at a round table in a hotel conference room just off the pool, feeling disconnected from my classmates. They were content to chitchat; their conversation sounded like it was in a foreign language. I sat nibbling on taquitos and dip with what felt like a chute within me that ran deep down into hell and back up. I felt centuries older than everyone around me. It was exactly the kind of moment being wrapped in your arms would have comforted; I'd have found my center, cracked a smile, and carried on.

I thought I'd been doing better, had had enough standby modes where I could function adequately. But prom intensified my loneliness. You would've loved it, though. And I would have loved dancing with you. Though you weren't there in body, during our "awards ceremony," you were voted Biggest Teddy Bear. The applause was low-toned. I cried softly and excused myself to smoke a cigarette by the pool. I was voted Most Tele-pathic and Most Transpersonal. Had you been alive, that last award surely would have gone to you.

It was after prom that I became sick—deathly sick, you could say—and stayed in bed for five days with a fever and no voice. I was alone, with minimal communication with others and no food in the fridge. DVDs of *Friday Night Lights* were my only company. I loved those nights we'd cuddle in bed for hours and watch episode after episode. That show taught me what living in Oklahoma and Texas was like for you: dusty, small towns dominated by football and Christianity. While sick in bed I dared to watch season three—a season that hadn't yet aired while you were alive—and haunt myself with associations of you. As each episode started, the haunted, echoey theme song unleashed deeper grief. You used to smile at me, wave your gorgeous hands, and harmonize to the tune. With each episode, I plunged further into the flat, dry, Texas landscape and grew weaker as my vision got darker.

The show opened up the roughly patched vortex of pain I'd thought I moved through already. I mourned our past: innocent moments watching this show with you in bed. I mourned our future. We would never share a small house in the abandoned Texas countryside. No more two-stepping in the kitchen. No dream of riding horses together. No making love on a blanket in a field of wheat. No more pride at seeing my rugged, cowboy, football-champion of a man walking toward me on a dirt road.

No riding shotgun in a pickup. No sharing our daily lives. No more teammate, no more lover, no more companion. I felt too tired, too weak, too sick to fight the pain anymore. I couldn't go on one more day missing you. This time, Ben wasn't there to help me. No one was. I felt I was dying at the bottom of the ocean.

I imagined the ways I could end my life and return to you. Eating a poisonous plant seemed the most natural and easiest way to die. From bed I researched these deadly plants on the internet: castor bean, rosary pea, wolfsbane, bushman's poison, angel's trumpet. Poetic names for agents of death. I considered ordering some but knew I couldn't. I was stuck. And it wasn't fair. I lay in this sickened fog for days, until my body regained enough strength to move and sit outside on the front lawn in the June sunshine.

A few days later, Ben came over to play a recording of the three of us he'd found on his computer. It was an interview he'd conducted for his couple's therapy class over a year earlier. I had put off listening to it because I was scared of how I would feel hearing your deep, rumbling voice again. I might unravel further, if that was possible. It was time, though; I wanted to hear it. Maybe it held clues as to why I wasn't enough of a reason for you to stay. Ben wasn't going to let me listen to it alone. He came over for moral support.

Your voice was deep and soothing, like I remembered it. Full of heart. But I didn't cry. I intentionally kept a clinical distance, analyzing the content and process of the interview like I did with my clients. You didn't say much. I noticed I answered the questions at length, and passion filled my voice. Then there was you. You didn't match any of it. There wasn't anything you said or any tone in your voice that met my passion, enthusiasm, and commitment to our relationship. Don't get me wrong—you had some lovely, sweet things to say. But you often responded with one-word answers that sounded like you were holding back what you really felt or thought. At times it seemed you were answering with what you thought I wanted to hear. For the first time, I could hear how afraid you were, how you avoided being honest about your real feelings. You used your diplomatic skills, your acting talents, and your spiritual views to bypass feeling romantic love and making a commitment to me. You hid behind the smokescreen of your "spiritual path" and used it to avoid being honest and authentic, with me or with anyone. I realized just how wounded and incapable you truly were—how much fear of intimacy and connection you lived with. Every topic and question had a way of being about you and going back to you as you avoided the truth, stumbling through your mental mazes of confusion, searching for a way out, an answer. I know you were not consciously or maliciously intending to do this or be this way. But the fact is, you chose to hold yourself back from me. You avoided life and loving me.

And then there was me. My heart melted with compassion for myself and for the ways I loved you, for how much I tried and for how much I had lost. I had struggled ruthlessly to learn your more "spiritual" way of life, to help you feel safe, and make it okay for you to share all of yourself with me, even your dark, ugly parts. Look what you left me with in return. Our relationship was imbalanced. I would do *anything* for you. I'd give up my life to be with you. You wouldn't do the same.

While listening to the recording, I realized I deserved and deserve so much better than your abandonment. In some ways you weren't worthy of my love, devotion, commitment, and support. You didn't in any way, shape, or form reciprocate my feelings. I have been beating myself up for not being there for you, but it was *you* who wasn't there for *me*. You didn't stop for a single second to consider my feelings when you put yourself in front of a train. You were too self-involved to care about how I would feel after your death. Wasn't I enough of a reason for you to stay?

The next afternoon, as I zipped down the street to grab an iced coffee in between clients, I was flooded with adrenaline. The questions were these: How long was I going to continue making sacrifices for men who weren't there for me? Was I really going to keep prioritizing you as the be-all, end-all of my existence and throw my life away, following you into death, when you hadn't even considered my feelings when you killed yourself? I had poured myself into you, loved you hugely. Your death had made me lose myself—swallowed me up in grief and after-life codependency. I had stopped valuing who I was and all I had to offer. Instead, I fell into my usual pattern of being led by men, of giving up myself or parts of myself to be with the man I loved. I was once again being led by you. How far was I going to take this? I would've given up my life to be with you. Would you have done the same for me? Obviously not. You couldn't even meet me halfway when you were alive. What had you done for me that wasn't ultimately about you? Kill myself for you? Hell no. Not anymore. When you killed yourself, I'd let you steal my power. I wanted it back.

I began to see myself. This whole time, I'd only been seeing you. And now I'd been snapped into clarity. I was the one who was all the things you were not. I was strong, capable, immensely loving, deeply passionate, honest, fearless, and selfless. All the virtues and strengths that you lacked, I have. From that day on, my focus shifted from you to me. I was the one who kept me company through those dark months, not you. I knew myself to the core. I know how worthy I am and how I want to be with a man deserving of all I have to offer, a man who can love as intensely as I do and who will be as dedicated and committed as I am. Even though you too had told me this, it was the first time I felt it and could envision myself with a man other than you. I finally let go of some of my idealization of you and my longing to be with you at all costs. The breakthrough made me excited to dive into my life and be as fully human as possible. I felt eagerness for the fucking amazing life I knew I was going to have. Hey, I thought, if I can survive this, I can survive anything.

My feet were finally cemented to the ground. I wanted to reach up, squeeze life in my fists, and embody everything I am. I wanted what's mine—what I'd never even glimpsed, let alone touched, before. I wanted to fulfill my purpose and live up to my highest potential, not sell myself short or deny myself anything ever again, especially not for any man. And just like that, I was released from my prison and found my drive to live again. I rolled up my proverbial sleeves and, with a swivel of my hips, strutted back to work.

The process of mourning—of bleeding and oozing my guts and heart all over the floor—is helping me become familiar with my insides and reassemble them into something new; it's like I've died and am being reborn a better version of myself. I know myself now.

You were real. Your love was real. I still love you as much as when you were alive, perhaps more.

Sarah

DATE: DECEMBER 31, 2010
SUBJECT: MINING GOLD IN HELL

....

Dear John,

Finding purpose, finding meaning in my loss has been my lifeline. It's the only thing that's kept me going and organized me up from being a puddle of pain lying at the bottom of the abyss and into a functioning, spirited, driven human being. How can I find meaning and purpose in your death and begin to tell a new story, over and over again, about my life and the reasons I've had to endure what I'm experiencing? There is a real purpose for me being here at this time, this place. My heartache, my loss, my grief, my pain is molding me into a new version of myself. Whether I feel it or not. I'm trying to uncover the gold, my gifts and strengths that have been hiding in the shadows for so long. I'm so close to them now. What are they? How can I use them? What can I do with them? What can I do with them to make my life a better one, an exalted version of the one I used to live?

How can I live up to the highest designs of my being? How can I use what I'm experiencing to be of service to others? How can I make the pain worthwhile and echo out through the annals of history? I may not know the answers now; the pain is too deep and the darkness too blinding, but I keep fumbling one foot forward, one step at a time, and more will be revealed in time. I won't let my loss be in vain.

Yours,
Tiger

···

Dear John,

This is new territory for me. I had thought that I'd moved through a lot of grief these past two years, but something's bubbling up and SOMETHING funky is rearing its ugly head. This time it feels different. It's new. I've changed and so my way of seeing and feeling this loss has changed. I'm noticing anger and irritability at you. For the way you treated me in many respects. Bothered and almost disgusted by the way you abandoned me without consideration for our relationship or me. Resentful, again, that you weren't able to appreciate me as I want to be appreciated. A lot of issues that I have/had with men in general are now being projected onto you because of your ultimate abandonment and betrayal. You basically shattered my trust in men. Though these feelings and thoughts are not new, they are coming up now in different ways. Lots of stress, chaos, and anger. I'm so sick of this, of how your death keeps fucking me up. I'm afraid that after all the damage has been totaled up, reviewed, and healed, I'm still going to end up alone. "The fucked up spinster semi-widow who just had so much Potential." "Too bad John killed himself. She never recovered or loved again." The End.

And yet I still idealize you. I still love you. I still feel compassion and sorrow for your struggles and your life. I find myself flooded with grief and tears at the oddest moments. Having a hard time speaking about it and about you to others without tearing up. Having a hard time speaking about it to myself in my head without feeling sad and teary. So many conflicting, complicated emotions and ideas are vying to be seen and heard and are intersecting with one another in new ways. It's hard to describe or explain, but feels like a new perspective is molding—beyond my control.

—Ms. Havisham

Well, you should know. You were there and you put me there. I
have you to thank for the endless, claustrophobic darkness that is
my life. Sometimes I'm a mermaid and I play with beings down
in the water. It's fun, girly, mystical, sexy, trendy, whatever. Us
mermaids, we dive deep. But swimming down there for me feels
like drowning. I'm drowning at the bottom of the ocean, waiting
for the next wave to move through, for something to change. I
swim up to the surface sometimes and catch some sun. I breathe.
I live a sort of normal existence amongst the humans. I try to
date. I fail. None of these guys can compare to your beauty.
They don't have your blue eyes. Your sweetness, your laughter.
They treat me like shit, somehow, in the end. I don't understand
how. How I didn't see it, how I chose a douchebag, again, to treat
me like shit. But none of them hurt me half as badly as you. You
ripped out my heart and sank me down, down, down to a place
below the earth where breathing and seeing is hard, gasping
with eyes sewn shut. Wheezing, adjusting to my life without
you. It's been years. I swam back up to the surface a while and
hung out there for some time. Swimming out of that dark, inky,
thick water took all my energy, all my time. I learned to move
my arms, I picked up pieces of my shattered heart. I put them
back together and when I got back up to the surface, I warmed

myself up. And I tried. But what's the point. I still can't see and now I meet with men who tell me to move my seat as soon as I meet them on a date. I waste my feelings on dicks who promise to visit and are "so excited to see me" but then don't make their flight because they've been a "slacker." I can't break out of my patterns no matter how much fucking work I do and how hard I try. I can't see clearly. And it's all your fault. I blame you for fucking up my heart and my life. Sure, I have great things going for me that I've created, but underneath the surface I'm scarred in a way that I don't think can be fixed. And I hate you. I want to hate you. I want you to know that you fucking ruined my life and I'm not going to make spiritual excuses for why you left or get lost in bullshit "spiritual contracts" that you and I had or in trying to understand your suicidal motives any longer. You were a fucking confused selfish bastard. Yes, you played us all as fools for loving your bright light and your warm spirit and your hugs. Fuck your hugs. You lied to all of us and you damaged me and your family most of all. We will never get over what you did. We will never stop missing you, you fucking asshole. I hate you and I miss you and I hate that I have such a hard time hating you. It's lonely down here in the dark underbelly of the ocean. There are weird snarly amoeba and little pricklies that bite me and crawl over me, the brownish seaweed wraps around me, ensnaring my throat, locking me down. I can't breathe and I can't swim away anymore. There's nowhere else to go; the world has caught up to the darkness and I can't find my usual escape routes anymore. I think my vision is getting clearer. I'm seeing things I've never seen before. These creatures are ugly, radiated, potbellied blue bulgy-eyed fish. I don't like them. I'm scared. But I've nowhere to go. I'm going to blame you again for all of this. You're my target for my dark underwater vision of the ugly creatures of the sea; we're drowning together and I'm turning into one as we speak. You left me here to drown and I hate you for it. Fuck you. You ruined my life. I can't wait to see you again and punch you in the face. This is what your fucking selfishness has caused. How ya gonna help me now? Huh? What else is there to say? I don't think I'm ever going to truly love again or trust another man in my heart. I'll just keep pushing them away for my own entertainment, to pass the time. I'll just find flaw after flaw in them and keep on going with my abandonment drama until I die and then I see you again and I punch you in the face. And I may become a lesbian because I don't feel safe around men. I don't trust them. And you're to blame. You suck, John. I wish you had been more of a hero and stuck around and faced your fears and let us help you. You caused more damage then you know and I hope you're up there doing repentance or community service or whatever the fuck you do up there to make up for your stupid suicides. So yeah, this is what it feels like at the bottom of the fucking ocean.

-Sarah

the map:
guidance for shifting

Grappling with regret and guilt is the most common emotional cluster you'll be wrestling with, especially initially: wishing you could have done more or said just the right thing at the right time to save your beloved. We all go through this and take ownership and responsibility for their death, when in fact the ownership and responsibility for their suicide is completely on them. You could *not* have saved them. And that is a hard, cold truth that you need to understand and drill into your mind. *Nothing* you could have done would have reversed the pain and darkness that led them to suicide. If someone is determined to die, he will find a way to make that happen. I beat myself up for years, believing that if only I had acted as John's "security guard" and followed him around and stayed up nights protecting him, maybe he would have lived. Or if I only had gotten him a sleeping pill sooner, then he would have felt more rested, less sleep deprived, and could have stayed alive. If only I had asked him point-blank if he was suicidal and did he have a plan for enacting his suicidal fantasies, then I could have had him hospitalized against his will and he would have lived. If only.

None of these options are viable; none would have significantly helped to stabilize John. And the same is true for your *if onlys*. They wouldn't have panned out the way you're convincing yourself they would have.

You are not responsible for your beloved's suicide. To feel as if you are is codependent thinking, and will hurt you and keep you pining for an alternate ending. It makes you overly responsible for someone else's life and free will. Recognize your own humanness and powerlessness. Deeply feel it on an emotional and cellular level. You don't have control. You can't play god. This will humble you and bring you to your knees at the fucking unfathomable mystery of it all.

USE YOUR ANGER

Your anger will be your primary driver out of hell. Use it as fuel to give you power over this powerless situation. Your breakthroughs about your life and your worth lie on the other side of anger. And so, like the other emotions that occur within grief, allow yourself time to fully feel it and express all of it. Sometimes it may not look pretty, but let the anger out as much as you can (as long as it's not on other people). This could mean journaling, dancing, screaming, playing aggressive sports, boxing, hitting your bed with a bat, expressing anger at your therapist, and/ or simply sitting with your anger and allowing it to be there during meditation.

Some people jump to anger quickly and start directing that anger toward their beloved. Others do not and, rather, get consumed by sadness. Either way is fine and normal, but if you don't have access to your anger, it's something to reflect on and consider. Perhaps listen to some badass angry songs that connect you to it. Or practice screaming, having a tantrum, just for the sake of it, until you connect to the anger in your body through your voice. If you're a person who is quick to anger, make sure that you don't bypass feeling sad and get stuck in your anger. Without processing the sadness underneath your anger, you may get stuck in what is called "toxic anger"—anger that is anger for anger's sake and keeps you looping and indefinitely angry. This is a manifestation of unresolved grief. If this is the case with you, make sure you are working through it with a professional and processing some of the other emotions.

Either way, you are completely entitled to feel angry. Suicide and/or the death of a loved one is an incredibly unjust and unnatural circumstance to be dealing with, especially if you're young. While death is a natural part of life, losing our loved one through death is so finite, incomprehensible, and not an easily adaptable experience. Even if your beloved leaves a suicide note and you have clarity on why he killed himself, there are still so many questions left unanswered, conversations left unspoken, and mysteries left unsolved that we may never get closure or resolution on. This incompleteness is maddening.

Feeling abandoned may also generate anger. How could he do this to me? How dare she do this to me? What's wrong with me that he did this to me? Why wasn't I enough for her to stay? Who will ever love me again now that I'm so damaged? The feeling of being abandoned by your beloved may make you angry at him or her. You have every right to these feelings, and you have every right to be angry with your beloved for causing this. They did cause this unfortunate trauma in your life. Period. End of story. If you can truly absorb those last two sentences, you will feel your anger. This is not to play the blame game, but rather to help you see the objective cause and effect of the matter. This is why people who take their own lives leave so much damage in their wake.

PRACTICE SELF-FORGIVENESS

Forgiving yourself for not saving your beloved is key. There are many books to read on forgiveness. Dr. Fred Luskin, a Stanford researcher who was also my dissertation chair, has written one of the foremost books on forgiveness, *Forgive for Good,* which can provide an access point into this process. What works for me is going into a meditative state and dropping into the sadness in my heart and letting my own humanity, fragility, and acceptance of myself soothe my need for control and my anger. A specific meditation that I practice and use with clients is in the Transformational Practices section at the end of this book.

DEVELOP A DAILY MEDITATION PRACTICE

In this day and age, I tell all my clients, if you don't have a regular meditation practice, you're putting yourself at risk for anxiety and depression. Meditation is an ancient practice whereby we cultivate the capacity and the muscle for sitting with discomfort, pain, and suffering without reacting to it unconsciously and, in doing so, letting it run our lives. By actually sitting and being with the pain and the grief, we allow the energy and the emotion to move. It will dissipate and shift on its own, but only if we first sit with it and give the pain permission to be there.

When it comes to grief, sitting with the pain often will provoke tears and crying. This is a good thing. You want this to happen; it's our body and soul's natural way of releasing the sorrow. By being able to feel your sorrow and release it through tears and meditation, you are developing strength and courage—and strength and courage are the qualities you need to get through this darkness. You cannot truly navigate the dark without them. I urge you to start meditating as a way to strengthen yourself so you can better handle your loss. You will need inner strength to get through this. Even if you only meditate for five minutes a day, it's worth the practice. (I've listed key meditation books and teachers in the Resources section at the end of this book.)

SHIFT YOUR PERSPECTIVE ON DEATH AND LIFE AFTER DEATH

One of the approaches that most greatly helped me start to decrease my grief about John's suicide and also my fear of death was to challenge the programming of our world—the messaging that tends to be more scientifically based and touts the idea that death is the final end to life and nothing exists beyond it. If I believed in this point of view, I would have felt even more terrified, grief-stricken, and despairing. It simply was not acceptable to me that death was the end of John and the end of life.

I've always been fascinated by perspectives that advocate that there's more to existence than just a body, and I've read a lot about near-death experiences (NDEs) and even explored having my own conscious out-of-body experiences when I was younger. I've long been willing to believe that we have a life beyond the body. I've also had many psychic phenomena happen to me in my life—like when, on the night he died, I felt John's presence in my bedroom. It was such a soothing feeling, and even though I couldn't necessarily see him with my eyes, I had to believe that it was still him. From there, I knew I needed to strengthen my psychic abilities so that I could continue to connect with him on the other side. This was one of my only driving impetuses in the early days after his death: *How can I develop and cultivate my abilities and my faith so that I can still communicate and connect with John?* Cultivating faith was key, as my rationally driven mind easily doubted that what I was feeling or hearing was actually John.

I write at greater length about this in the Transformational Practices section at the end of the book. But for now, at this stage in your healing, simply know that it's important to start the shift toward connecting with your beloved on the other side, and also knowing that he/she isn't gone for good.

There are several ways in which I went about cultivating my awareness about life after death and connecting with John. In the pages to follow, I'll explore each one.

cultivating psychic abilities: clairaudience, clairvoyance, clairsentience

If you even mildly believe in these kinds of things, it's helpful to start cultivating your extrasensory abilities so that you can begin to explore communicating with your beloved on the other side. Start to explore which "clair" you're more naturally prone to. I took a quiz through a site called Inner Expansion and determined that I'm more sensitive to hearing and feeling psychic information. Once that was established, I bought books and did research on how to cultivate these muscles. In the ensuing months, I did exercises and talked to John each morning in my meditation practice, and waited for his responses. I also kept journals and notes about all the signs I perceived to be from him.

seeking a medium, challenging our beliefs about life after death

Consulting with a highly-skilled, well recommended and vetted medium is a tremendously powerful way to crack through your beliefs about life after death. Once again, though, the medium has to be the real deal. Consulting with a charlatan or less-skilled medium can cause damage. So please, make sure that the medium you find comes referred by people you trust. See the resources appendix for places to start.

With the right medium, you will get specific communication from your beloved. You may even get answers as to why they killed themself. Getting this information is invaluable. Connecting to them on the other side brings an indescribable feeling of comfort, relief, and bliss. This experience helps you understand that there is no such thing as death, and that you have a community of loved ones on the other side who are looking out for you at all times. The boundaries between this reality and that one start to blur, and an incredible feeling of awe and the miraculous starts to saturate your being. This is healing.

finding evidence for life after death, and keeping track of signs and synchronicities

The first year or two following your beloved's death can feel surreal and have a magical quality as you're sorting out what happened. Invite the magic and the surreal. Ask your beloved, god, higher power, the universe, etc. to amp up the magic, the odd signs and synchronicities, from the other side. Then pay attention to them. Write them down in a journal.

These signs could be anything: songs that you and your beloved loved and had an inside connection with; specific animals or insects (dragonflies, bees, ladybugs) that have meaning for the two of you; lights flickering; candles going out; objects out of place; random people saying things that sound out of context yet oddly specific for you. Ask your loved one for a song and put your music on shuffle and see what shows up. Pay attention and take note of all of it. By noticing these moments and signs, you're cultivating a different awareness—one infused with spirit and the interconnected flow between this reality and your beloved's reality. And with a written-down collection of these signs, you're building more evidence for your rational mind to start to loosen its grip on death being a finite, black-and-white phenomenon.

connecting with your beloved through ritual, ceremony, and shamanism

Setting up an altar space dedicated to your beloved and a daily meditation practice is a sacred way of tuning into your beloved in spirit and honoring them. Rituals of various sorts, such as lighting candles, spending time in nature, shamanic ceremonies, baths, and more are channels of connecting and moving through stages of mourning. Working with a shaman or spiritual guide who can facilitate your awareness of other states of consciousness can help shift your perspective on the finality of death. (I talk about this more extensively in the Transformational Practices appendix.)

meaning-making

Much research on grief suggests that a great source of comfort is found in making some kind of meaning out of your loss. Finding a silver lining of some sort and creating a story or reason this suicide happened and what you can do with your life because of it is helpful as you attempt to take steps forward.

For me, it was essential to construct a narrative about why I am here on this planet, and to give purpose to this experience. I also have to *feel* my purpose as a higher calling. What I've identified as one of my purposes for being here without John is to help others who are going through this kind of tragedy. It was also crucial for me in those early years that I tell myself that once I completed my purpose in life, I would reunite with John. I wouldn't be alive a minute later or earlier than the moment that my soul has fulfilled its purpose. This narrative got me through those first two really dark years. I was able to stay busy and engaged, rushing to do my work and reach John.

My meaning-making stories have changed over the years as I've changed, and now my life is no longer about reaching John but about fulfilling my creative passions. Find a reason, whatever reason you need, in order to get through the dark. It doesn't matter if others believe your reasons. What matters is that it directs your sense of identity and purpose and keeps you moving.

Some questions for reflection are:

- Why is this happening in my life?
- What are the lessons here? Is there a recurring theme in my life?
- What does my soul need/crave?
- How can I transform this pain to help others?
- What is the next level of my surrender to this experience?
- How will I be different once I am on the other side of my grief?
- What can I offer others because of this hardship?
- What do I want my life to be about from here on out?
- What am I holding on to or resisting from my old life and old way of being?
- What am I afraid will happen, or won't happen if I surrender to this death?

therapeutic bodywork

Our feelings get stored and trapped in our bodies. Hopefully, you're seeing a trauma specialist who can facilitate the release of trauma from your nervous system. On top of this, it can be helpful to receive therapeutic bodywork that can move the stuck emotions and energy stored in your body. Because you are grieving, your body keeps getting flooded with emotion, much like a stretch of shore that's subjected to waves crashing in and out. There's a reason grief is so often likened to waves. The emotions keep ebbing and flowing. Bodywork is a great way to soothe yourself as you undergo this daily onslaught.

practices and outlets

You may not feel like you have energy for anything other than going to work or school and then home to sleep. That's completely normal. At some point, however, you may feel like you want to start channeling your energy into something more. This could be a good time to explore different modes of self-expression or practices.

After several months of grieving, I resumed my regular weekly dance practice. I also started riding horses, writing this book, and working on my dissertation. These activities force you into the moment, out of your head, and onto experiencing life in new ways. See what might be interesting to you. Even the smallest baby steps can move you forward.

beauty

Beauty is the new way of seeing and experiencing the world around me and within myself. Beauty is a quality of the heart and spirit, a mystical awareness, a way of being that I never intentionally sought to find yet emerged naturally as I began healing.

In the book of Isaiah, the prophet promises those in mourning "beauty for ashes, the oil of joy for mourning." When I heard those words, I lit up in recognition of what I'd been experiencing in my intense grief. I felt comforted; my pain was validated by those ancient words. But here's my disclaimer: if, while feeling suicidal after John died, someone had told me that if I just moved through the grief, life would feel qualitatively different in a positive way once I reached the other side of it, I'm not sure I would've believed her or even cared. So this section is a gentle invitation to you—a suggestion of a possible effect that may emerge once the darkness of grief has transmuted and lifted and you've discovered the hidden gems within yourself.

....

Dear John,

On Valentine's Day I gave a presentation about eighteenth-century Romanticism and included *The Sorrows of Young Werther* to illustrate how inherently beautiful experiencing longing and pain can be. Perhaps it was my way of sending you an encoded message, though I had for the most part given up on you. Afterwards you told me my presentation was an "experience." Remember that? And then in your passive, shy way, totally taking me by surprise, you asked what I was doing later. After weeks of distracting myself with other men and other things, I still had a thing for you, of course; your beauty was hard to ignore on such a daily basis. When you said you'd call me later with the plans, my old hope flickered and my stomach did a little leap.

I waited in front of the Italian restaurant in downtown Mountain View. Your favorite place, you'd told me when you called. I wore jeans, a black sweater, and those black and red earrings I bought in Paris that you'd complimented me on earlier, after class. You showed up a few minutes late in a whirlwind, looking determined. Your hair was freshly washed and styled in carefully twirled ringlets. You were also wearing black—a rugged

145

semi-zip cardigan that showed off your shoulders and your slender waist. You took my hand as if it were the most natural thing in the world and guided me toward the back of the restaurant to introduce me to the owner. He wasn't there. You stood for a second, your light blue eyes pondering.

"You know, I think this place is a little too noisy," you said. "Let's go somewhere else. I know of this other place where we'll be able to hear each other talk." You took my hand again and breezed me out of the restaurant. A certain energy buzzed in the air, and it felt like we were on an adventure.

We took your car, a silver Pontiac Vibe. You opened the door for me, chivalrously. Your car was filled with a thick air of peacefulness and comfort. It even smelled relaxing, like laundry detergent. You drove stick, but I barely noticed your arm moving back and forth, your movements were light and graceful. You drove with flair. As a Manhattanite who didn't drive until age twenty-six, I notice how men drive and find it a huge turn-on. Clearly, you had been driving for a while. You said you learned on the backcountry roads of your farm in Oklahoma when you were twelve. Wow. Before I knew it, you slid into a spot and parked. You walked around, opened my door, and took my hand again.

"Okay, mademoiselle, here we go."

We walked past three houses, down a path lined with fragrant shrubs and statuesque redwood trees, and up to a door framed by a tree that sparkled with white Christmas lights. You opened the door and guided me into the house.

My eyes were bright with wonder. The lights were off but for a warm fire roaring in the fireplace and two candlesticks on the table, which was set for two. I shivered slightly with excitement.

Really? I wondered to myself. You did this for me? After all the confusion and rejection, you had cooked up this romantic Valentine's Day surprise. I so wanted to ask where this change of heart was coming from but didn't want to break the spell.

"Wow, John. This is so sweet." I kissed you on the cheek. You blushed, and then, with an air of confidence, escorted me to the table. You pulled out my chair and pushed me in.

"Can I get you a pillow for your back?" you asked. Before I had the chance to answer, you ran to the couch and plucked one and tucked it behind my back.

"I think you might need another one," you wondered aloud and quickly fetched a second pillow.

"Uh, okay, sure. I don't know . . ." I said, confused.

"Let me fix your chair. Excuse me for a minute."

I watched with a smile as you helped me up and then rearranged my chair with the extra pillow.

"That's better," you said as you pushed me in again.

You lit more candles, put on the soundtrack to an Almodovar film, and opened a bottle of red wine. You poured our glasses, then disappeared and came back a moment later with a red rose. Your mouth curled shyly as you handed it to me. Finally, you sat down across from me.

"Happy Valentine's Day, Sarah."
I pinched myself. Was this really happening?

We sipped our wine, and you stared at me, intently and sweetly, with those big, innocent eyes that melted me every time. I felt shy and looked away. When you left for the kitchen for a few minutes, I gazed around. So this was where you lived, where you did hundreds of little idiosyncratic and cute things throughout the day that only your housemates had the pleasure and the privilege of glimpsing. The room was warm and cozy, like dark chocolate. Next to a floral- patterned couch, a basket of knitting exuded a homey friendliness. The walls were hung with oil paintings of people I didn't know yet; a grand piano occupied a corner, covered in doilies, dried flowers, and family photos. The mantel was adorned with photographs and statues of spiritual teachers, Buddha, Chinese dragons, crystals, and incense. A plaque on the wall was dedicated to the memory of a pet mouse, Wally.

You whisked back in with two bowls of salad, disappeared, and came right back with five bottles of salad dressing. Then you were off again and returned quickly with five more dressings. You explained each dressing and lined them up in a neat row. It seemed important to you that I have every available option that could possibly be to my liking. I laughed with appreciation.

"Okay, John-— I got it., I'm okay with this one," I said as I picked out the Soy Sesame Asian Delight.

"Perfect," you said, with obvious pleasure.

I picked at my salad but couldn't eat. You served the main course of homemade meatballs and spaghetti with love and care, and I watched with delight every time you placed a plate in front of me. Your food was delicious, but I had no appetite. Waves of excitement, love, and nervousness rolled through my gut, translating into nausea. Eating was not an option.

You were a complete mystery to me, so light, warm, and loving, I didn't get it. I had to ask.

"John, do you have a dark side?"

Your eyes widened.

"A dark side? What do you mean?"

"I mean, have you ever done anything that's not right? Have you ever gotten depressed? Really angry? Have you ever broken rules? Done drugs? Smoked cigarettes? Thought about death? Known what it's really like in the deepest, darkest parts of your mind or had a dark secret that you haven't told anyone? I mean, you're so light and loving, I just gotta know if there's other darker things underneath."

After pondering this like it was a foreign concept, you admitted that you had felt a bit of anger and sadness on occasion, but no, for the most part, you didn't have a dark side.

This was a strange revelation to me. It seemed impossible. Everyone has a vice, a temper, a tattoo, a little contempt. But your answer felt honest.

As we ate and drank, it was so easy to get a sense of you without other people around. There was more to you than I could even imagine.

During the main course, your housemates Barbara and Jean arrived home.

"Hello loves," you called in your deep voice.

They came in to say hello. You leaped up to embrace them in big hugs. Barbara was from England; she spoke with a proper accent and had twinkling, youthful blue eyes. Jean, with the short bowl haircut, spoke with strength and tenacity, using language that seemed to come from another century. I found out later she was a poet. They shared their home with you and Barbara's two older sons, Anthony and Malcolm, who were nowhere to be found that night. You left to check on something in the kitchen.

"Sarah, honey, so nice to finally meet you," Barbara said.

"Oh, thank you. It's nice to meet you, too, and see where John lives."

"Sarah, John is the most loving person I have ever known," Barbara said, straight out, in her stern English accent.

"Really?" I took a sip of wine, swallowing the information I'd already partly known.

"Honest to god."

You came back in the room and glanced at our plates.

"Mademoiselle, it's time for your dessert." With a quick, smooth movement you flicked your wrists, removed our plates, and then disappeared back into the kitchen.

A few minutes later, you waltzed back in and placed down a glass dish full of perfect scoops of chocolate ice cream garnished with two chocolate truffles. You also gave me the option, just in case I wanted it, to add chocolate or caramel sauce, or both.

Chocolate was still on my lips when you extended your hand and asked me to dance. Your body was warm and you smelled fresh— like a mix of wildflowers, sunscreen, and seaweed by the ocean. We danced slowly and smoothly to our own rhythm. Heaven is a dance floor with you on it. The atmosphere shifted and the room disappeared. My questions, my up-and-down hope and struggles to get over you, the distance, the confusion, all disappeared. Everything felt right. My heart was pounding. Our faces were inches apart. I could feel your breath. I turned my face and kissed you fully on the mouth. Like an extension of our dance, the kiss was graceful and natural. You kissed me back. My arms went around your neck, pulling you in, and wow. Your arms wrapped around my body, finally, the way they were meant to be. We stood lost in this first kiss, kissing and kissing, oblivious to the world. When you finally drove me back to my car, we kissed for another hour before I dreamed my way home.

John, it was the most delicious and romantic night of my life. I melted into feeling, maybe even believing, this was real. You were real. And everything I had felt for the last four and half months had been real; you had finally realized it. I loved being lead by the hand into your magical realm. You existed somewhere else, a place full of love, sweetness, and an indescribable, warm feeling of ease and gentleness. My rough edges were softening. I felt the pull to lose myself and dissolve. I told myself to stay grounded so I didn't float away with you.

I wish I had. I'd be in a better world right now.

Thank you for that perfect evening. The memory fills me with love.

Sarah

....

Dear John,

The night we celebrated the end of our first year of classes was
magic. Sky clear, air warm, we got drunk on margaritas and fell
backwards into a bed of pink petunias in downtown Mountain
View. With my big red and black poncho from Ecuador covering us, it was like a slumber party in the middle of the street.
People rolled their eyes and walked on by but we got cozy and
laughed and laughed as we stared up at the twinkling stars.
Once the absurdity subsided, the calm of the night sky set in.
We danced our way back to your house like two carefree spirits.
Since the night of your birthday, I'd wanted to dance home with
you through the trees. And so we did. Sometimes I have to pinch
myself so those days don't feel like a dream.

Once school was out, you flew to Oklahoma for a week to visit
with your mom, Tom, and Scott. You left me a voicemail in your
low voice and thick drawl:

"Hey Tiger. This is your personal cowboy calling. I'm standing
on top of a tractor trying to get reception and I wanna say I love
you. I want you. And I'm grateful for you in the world, for always
knowing what's best for you, and for speaking your truth."

I listened to your message over and over. You'd been quick to give me my pet name, Tigerlily: "fierce like a tiger on the outside and soft and yummy like a flower on the inside," you'd said. I, on the other hand, struggled to find the right one for you. I still don't have it. Cutie of a Cowboy never quite fit . . .

After Oklahoma, you flew to Texas to spend a few days with your dad and stepmom, Sue-Ann. I met you at the airport in Dallas for a weekend of fishing with you and your dad. You strolled through the terminal at Dallas Love Field. Your pale, honey-colored hair was loose and messy from the humidity and you wore a red-and-blue-plaid western snap shirt, faded blue jeans, running shoes, and a straw cowboy hat. Such a friggin' hunk.

The night was hot and sticky. It was my first time in Texas. The city seemed to pulse with thickness and expectancy. Sharing it with you was like living a dream I'd never quite known I'd had. Your dad Harry, and your eighteen-year-old half sister, Betty-Sue, picked us up. Harry was tall, with a red, weathered face, sunken blue eyes, a wide mouth, and grey-brown hair. He had large, strong hands and elegant wrists like yours. Betty-Sue stood plump with a button nose, shaggy brown hair, and glasses. You and she looked nothing alike. You and your dad hugged for a long time. Then he gave me a big long and unexpected hug. When he was finished, Harry gave me a quick look up and down. I was wearing tight jeans, a red tank top, and boots.

"Son, she sure is pretty," he said with a big, loopy smile.

We headed two hours north to a small country town called Winnsboro, where your dad had recently moved. After a long pit stop at the biggest Walmart I'd ever seen and a visit through the Taco Bell drive-thru, we arrived at your dad's house after midnight. He was profusely apologetic and self-conscious that the house was small and messy and explained he'd recently lost his job and just paid for Betty-Sue's wedding. To cut costs, they'd moved to this small, one-bedroom house, three rooms in all: a crowded living area, a small kitchen, and a darkened bedroom in the back. The living room was strewn with ugly brown furniture, garbage, to-go cups, and ashtrays full of cigarette butts. When we placed our bags of groceries on the kitchen table, hundreds of roaches ran for cover in all directions. We both pretended we hadn't seen them. When we cleared an area on the living room floor and laid down the air mattress, more roaches dispersed. Once down on the air mattress with the lights out, I clung to your body for refuge. As long as we were floating on our mattress and I was holding on to you, I felt safe from whatever was crawling in the dark around us. Your body was my life preserver, and I was soon able to drift into a nice sleep.

You were up at dawn, helping your dad load the lawn mower onto his truck. He was trying to establish his landscaping business in this new town and you went with him to mow lawns. The weather was overcast and balmy. I sat outside on a weed-lined patch of pavement with Sue-Ann and Betty-Sue. Between puffs on her ever-present cigarette, Sue-Ann told me she had been struck by lightning not just once, or twice, but seven times. She was afraid of the oncoming thunderstorm. Who could blame her?

Dogs barked off in the neighborhood. I shifted uncomfortably, trying to avoid being bitten by microscopic red bugs while I pumped Sue-Ann and Betty-Sue for information about you. They were happy to comply. They told me how as a teenager when you'd visit your pa, the girls in town would call and follow you around, but you didn't care much for them. You kept to yourself and helped your dad around the ranch (where they used to live) and studied your bible. Sue-Ann seemed mighty proud of you and proud to be related to you. She said there was no one else like you and called you "refreshing." I agreed.

The purpose of our trip was for you to bond with your dad over some world-class bass fishing. The next day, despite the hot stormy weather, we set out in the truck in the wee hours of dawn, stopped at a gas station to get our fishing licenses and a few ham sandwiches, then continued on to Lake Fork. Almost desperate to be of help, you ran to your dad's side at every step of the way. With much manly and technical maneuvering, the boat was unhitched and eased into the lake. You knew what you were doing. This confident, rugged side was not the man I usually saw sitting in front of a computer at graduate school in California. It was impressive and hot.

When we pushed off from shore, thunderstorms were on their way. The sky was large and grey; the air was so electric it sparkled. As we floated on the black water, I saw the beauty of that single moment in time and felt an enormous sense of joy at being able to share it with you.

Soon enough, the rain came down in cold streaks. You and I huddled under my favorite rainbow-colored sarong from Brazil as your dad sped back to the dock. After ten minutes of roaring wind and splashing, we reached the dock. You helped your dad hook the boat to the truck; your tan, veiny forearms were taut and defined under the strain of pulling. I made it a little difficult for you because in that moment I couldn't stop myself from grabbing you toward me and kissing your face dearly in the rain. Your masculinity, humility, and love for your father filled me with passion and appreciation for you. You were a bit bashful about kissing me in front of your dad but eventually gave in. You smelled sweet, like fresh vanilla, and I took you in with all my senses. Kissing you in the rain in Texas . . . that was amazing.

We sought shelter at the little restaurant by the lake with a sign for pie. "Now that's what I'm talkin' about! Mmhm," you said. Apparently, they served the best pie in the county and had thirty different flavors. We ordered your favorite, peanut-butter icebox. The place was air-conditioned; my wet hair was up in a bun, my skin was damp and covered in goose bumps; I sat on my hands and squirmed in my seat to stay warm. Chicken-fried steak was on the menu and I had to have it. It was strange, but I loved it because it was emblematic of Texas—a part of you. You left for the restroom.

"I know this might be none of my darn business, Sarah, but I'm gonna ask ya: do you think my son here's the one?" your dad said.

I smiled shyly, but was delighted with the question. "Yes. I do. He is the sweetest person I have ever met."

"Oh yes, he is. Always been like that. Popped out as loving and as sweet as you can imagine. Wouldn't speak a mean word about anyone. I'm just so happy he's found someone like you." You came back to the table.

"Son," your dad said, "I was just about to tell Sarah that you two make a fine and beautiful couple. I am real happy for ya son, for the both of ya."

You giggled boyishly and flashed me a smile. "Thank you, Dad. And I'm real glad that Sarah could come down and meet you."

"Oh son, it makes me so happy she's here. I can't begin to tell you." His voice choked as he turned to me. "I wonder how come you're visitin' with me and not his mom?"

"Well . . ." I paused, thrown a little off guard. "I don't know, I've heard a lot about you, and John invited me, so I figured why not?"

"I'm sorta surprised you'd want to meet me, I guess."

"No," I said and shook my head slowly. I didn't know what else to say.

The next day we were up at five thirty; it was a long, wet day of fishing in the rain. When we returned in the evening, we showered and got shiny for a nice double date of country dancing and karaoke with your dad and Sue-Ann. I wore my dark pink urban cowboy boots I'd gotten in San Francisco a while back and felt pretty good about them. You looked like a real Texan in your blue-and-brown-plaid western shirt and pale jeans.

The first dance hall was large, dark, and the music too loud. It was decked with deer heads, mounted fish, and blue and gold Bud and Coors Light signs, respectively. I saw lots of belt buckles, plaid shirts, and cowboy hats. I was totally smitten.

You held out your arm and asked me to two-step. I was flustered and intimidated by the hordes of couples with fancy, impeccable two-steps I'd never seen before. They floated across the floor too fast for me to even see what they were doing with their feet. You held me patiently and coached me with a soothing "One-two-two, one-two-two." It was obvious I was not from around there, but I kept up as best as I could. Then the DJ switched to the electric slide. I laughed as the whole crowd of adults executed the moves with gravity. But we sure slid with the rest of them.

At the next dance hall we ordered a pitcher of Coors Light, you and your dad's favorite. "Now that's what I'm talkin' about!" you hollered as you sipped.

You asked Sue-Ann to dance and led her around the floor. She was quite an excellent two-stepper. You were gallant; any mother's dream son. Your dad and I danced a bit, but we were not as adept and after a few laughs and stumbles we sat down to our beer.

You picked up the microphone and sang Johnny Cash's "Ring of Fire" and Ernie Ford's "16 Tons," which was one of your favorite songs. The large brown room was dark and mostly empty. You sang for yourself, not for us, staring into a distant corner, like you were proving something, but I don't know what. Sue-Ann remarked that your voice wasn't low enough to do Johnny. I disagreed. You were perfect. As you sang "16 Tons" your voice was rumbling and magnificent, lost on the empty room. That song still echoes in my mind often.

The next day was Father's Day, and I slept in while you went fishing with your dad. It was also our last day in Texas and we needed to be at the Dallas airport later to catch our eight o'clock flight. You returned early from fishing because your dad wanted to buy a lawn mower on sale at Sears. However, he had bad credit and no credit card. That afternoon he convinced Sue-Ann to open a credit card so he could get his lawn mower. They planned to be back at four o'clock to drive us to the airport, two hours away.

We were packed, bags ready by the door, at four. But there was no sign of your dad. By four thirty you had begun cleaning the house, rearranging the furniture, and fluffing the pillows. You kindly gave your dad a call. He had just gotten the credit card, he was almost at Sear's and would be round to pick us up soon, he said. You appeared relaxed and not at all anxious to be getting on the road. I, on the other hand, as you know, have anxiety about being on time, and I like to pace my schedule and give myself exactly the right amount of time so I am punctual (I think this is a New Yorker thing). I also tend to have anxiety about getting to the airport on time. Call me crazy, but I think most people do. When I heard the update about your dad's whereabouts, I didn't say anything, but my stomach and jaw tightened. I was counting on the fact that your dad would probably get lost once we hit Dallas and we needed to allot a sufficient amount of buffer time for getting lost and finding our way through the massive airport. Your response was to clean the kitchen, wash the dishes, and prepare a huge salad. By five o'clock, I was panicking. Where was he? Was he not aware of the fact that we had to get to the airport, it took two hours to get there, we were going to get lost, and we could miss our flight? It wasn't like we were just going to the movies and there'd be no consequences save missing the beginning if we showed up late.

You were lying on the couch, going in and out of napping and, I imagine, practicing being present. At five fifteen you called your dad and lovingly asked him where he was and if you needed to make arrangements for a taxi to take us to the airport. He said he was close by, around forty-five minutes away.

"Jesus Christ," I muttered.

Betty-Sue and Bobby rolled their eyes and shook their heads as if they'd seen this type of shenanigan before. When you got off the phone, you told us the plan: Sue-Ann was on her way back and she was going to drive us to a certain intersection twenty minutes away, where we'd meet up with your dad and he'd take us the rest of the way. Now we had to wait for Sue-Ann.

I sat outside the hot, stuffy house, trying not to show my irritation with your dad. Betty-Sue and Bobby were just as upset with him and told me story after story about how your dad frequently did things like this to Sue-Ann and the rest of the family. When Sue-Ann's mother passed away, your father didn't want to go out of state with her to Oklahoma for the funeral because they couldn't afford to both take off work. Sue-Ann went on her own to her mom's funeral. On the day of the funeral, your dad decided he missed Sue-Ann and flew to see her. He arrived in the middle of the service and started hollering and yelling, insisting she drive him back to Texas right then and there. They told me stories about your dad buying so many things on credit with no intention of ever paying it back and badgering Sue-Ann for years to get a credit card so he could use it. I listened as objectively as possible, as your stepsister and stepbrother-in-law were all too eager to defame your father to me. I watched as you stayed in the house and prepared a salad to-go for your dad and Sue-Ann. You showed no hint of anger or resentment. My heart began to break for you and the disappointments I imagined you'd endured with your father over the years—the loss of not being able to solidly rely on him to honor his commitments and come through for you. And still, through it all, you were humble and forgave, and remained an openly devoted son. Your love for your dad brought tears to my eyes. In that moment I felt grateful for my parents and their no-nonsense reliability. I know if they were to drive me two hours to the airport, they would revolve their whole day around getting me there, and not just on time but early. I could see my dad pacing around the house, waiting to leave. I guess we're from different cultures and we've developed norms and different senses of time. I felt a sad compassion for you and what you must have silently endured with your father.

Sue-Ann finally arrived home. We said our goodbyes quickly and got going. You gave Sue-Ann her salad and she was grateful for it. We reached the intersection and Sue-Ann and your dad switched vehicles. We were finally on the road by five fifty. I was beyond anxious at this point. How were we going to make our eight o'clock flight? I was tense, and I must admit I was angry with your dad for giving us the run-around and not being considerate of our time. Sitting in the backseat, I put on headphones and listened to my iPod to get control of myself. You presented your salad to your dad and told him the timing was working out perfectly and you were glad he was able to get everything done that he needed. You said you were sure we were going to make our flight and everything was going to be okay. You talked of how much you would miss him when you were back in California. The green Texas countryside rolled by and I cried for your beautiful kindness toward your father. I knew that if I were in your position and my dad picked me up for the airport two hours late, I probably would've been on the phone giving him attitude and saying some not-so-nice things. I wished I could be more like you, but I knew it was not the way I'm made and that pained me. You were tragically pure.

And I knew I was the luckiest girl alive to have the privilege to be with you and receive your love. That much I know is true. I also know your father was the luckiest father in the world to be blessed with a son who stood by him with utmost love, who followed him like a puppy dog, and doted on his every word while his other children were either not on speaking terms with him or blatantly complained, gossiped, and trashed him to anyone who would listen. No one has been more blessed than your dad to have a son like you. He didn't deserve you. Neither did I. Yet we were fortunate, somehow, to have you in our lives to light our paths with your unconditional understanding. Your dad and I have that in common.

I kept quiet, and as we got closer to the airport my stomach clenching finally ceased. I helped your dad navigate the big airport because we made a few wrong turns. Finally, we made it to the right place; the airport sidewalk was my safe harbor, and I heaved a sigh of relief as soon as my feet hit the pavement. It was seven twenty. We could still make it. I grabbed my bag and said a hurried goodbye to your dad and let you have a moment with him.

At the check-in counter, your eyes looked sunken and full of sadness.

"What's wrong?" I asked.

"I'm the scourge of the Earth," you said, looking down.

"No. John. You're the kindest person I know. You were amazing with your dad." I wanted to shake you and make you believe me.

"I know I have more work to do because I noticed some shame about my father come up," you said.

I wrapped my arms around you and hugged you fiercely. I wanted my love to take away your pain. I wished I could convey to you the beauty I'd seen and how much I'd learned about love from you in those few hours.

Sitting next to you on the plane, I held your hand like it was the most precious treasure in the world. An honor to sit by your side. Through tears, I shared my devotion with you. Here I was, a mere mortal, sitting in the presence of an angel whose loving nature brought me to my knees. I was grateful to be sitting next to you, to even call myself your girlfriend. It was almost laughable that I was. I was light years away from where you were spiritually, and perhaps I might never get there. But as the sun set fuchsia outside our window, it was simply enough to sit by your side and hold your hand while you drifted off into your precious sleep. I didn't take my eyes off you the whole way home.

John, my life has been blessed for having known you and seen your ways. I reach for your levels of love and compassion. I don't know if I can be as bighearted as you, but I now know what it looks like in human form.

Sweet dreams. I'll see you there.

Your Tigerlily

Dear John,

My old therapist in Palo Alto once warned me about you. "The brighter the light, the darker the shadow," he said in response to my gushing about you being so light and loving. I rolled my eyes at him. I hated those new-agey Jungian platitudes. What a bunch of psycho-babble. Besides, what did he know? If only he'd met you, then he'd understand.

Well, two and a half years after your shocking suicide, clearly I was wrong. The therapist was right. I understand this expression very well now. Your light and shadow were so extreme. How do I reconcile your indescribable celestial innocence and beauty with the violence and brutality of your self-inflicted death? It's like they cancel each other out, making you, and all of this, almost unreal. You imprinted these elements into me and now I must integrate these polarities within myself. Perhaps this is my soul's task here.

I've come to understand how the opposite of that statement is just as true: the darker the shadow, the brighter the light. The depths of our pain, anger, and sorrow are proportionate to our capacity to feel love, joy, and aliveness. The darkness reveals the light waiting for us on the other side of our suffering.

I once saw a video at the Suicide Prevention Center in Los Angeles honoring the survivors of suicide and the loved ones they'd loss. The smiles on the survivors' faces glowed unlike other people's; a stronger, brighter, and an unusual light radiated from their eyes. Staring a suicide in the face and living through one of the most incomprehensible kinds of death touches the deepest, darkest places in our soul. We live in that darkness for quite some time. When we emerge, nothing is the same. Joy is richer, laughter is deeper, and life feels juicier—so alive and palpable you can squeeze it in your fist. This aliveness is inherent in the pain itself. A high on life unlike anything else yet grounded, solid, and real. And trust me, given my life experiences growing up in the shadows, I'm the last person I'd ever expect to say this. John, your death killed me. I never would have anticipated feeling this lightness.

My new way of perceiving and experiencing the world is now my main way of being. And from time to time, significant markers, like the end of the creative process of this book or anniversaries, trigger lingering bubbles of grief. I imagine this will continue until my system has completely purged itself of all the grief, my old beliefs, and my old way of being. It could take months, years, or the rest of my life. My purging is a return to my innocence, the origin of it all. I'm reminded of a line from your suicide letter:

Somehow I have to believe that there is some original innocence within that transcends all.

My heart was broken open. I'm learning about what's inside, what delights me, and what feels painful. I'm learning to sing my own song and create a life of beauty and purpose. A life that is no longer about you and about getting to you but about the imaginings of my own heart. I'm snipping away the codependent cords that keep my happiness tied to you.

Bye for now,
Sarah

....

John,

Today on my way back from rollerblading by the beach in Santa Monica, walking barefoot in the sand, carrying a skate in each hand, I noticed a crowd of people gathered in a circle. Portable tables and folding chairs held in place by bags of food were set up a short distance away. A biker going by called out, "Is it a funeral?" I stepped a little closer to see. In the center of the crowd stood a man and a woman dressed in a white wedding dress. As I walked past, the group began to sing softly yet passionately:

"And we'll share this moment . . . together. And I'll always love you . . . forever." (You know, that song "Always & Forever," but with a lyric twist.)

It felt like some sort of sign. A low-maintenance wedding, abundant with love and harmony, and I happened to be walking by just at this precious moment. I did share the moment with them, together. What that sign means, I don't quite know.

I was never really a believer in signs or things like that, but after you passed on, my understanding of everything cracked. In my in-between-worlds state of grief, things that used to seem

166

mundane somehow, suddenly, magically, became imbued with spirit, with meaning and significance. Like the moment a bird flies across my path, or leaves fall on my head, the right song plays on the radio at the right time, or the wind blows as if in answer to a particular thought. These moments feel significant and interconnected with me, to me, and through me.

In the cracking of realities, life has shifted. The boundaries between this world and the other, the realm of spirit, became blurred. And in the depths of this fissure I could feel the pain of everyone and all the sorrow and suffering of the world. It swallowed me into hell, defying and daring me to hold on as tightly as I could for as long as possible, weeks, months, years, and the rest of my life.

The little things—the birds, the sun, the waves, the songs on the radio, the happenstance weddings I stumble upon, the ladybug at my feet, the flickering of lights in my room, the rainbows, the perfect movie my TV happens to be on when I turn it on—all have a mystical message for me. It's all significant. My year of magical thinking has become a life of magical seeing. And it's a bittersweet gift.

With love,
Sarah

....

Dearest John,

Acceptance of your death comes and goes. It's like I'm pieced back together with industrial-strength staples. Staples that will hold me together until I see you again and can dissolve into your warmth. I don't know how much more I can continue writing like this and looking back on my years of hell. My grief has lifted somewhat and I'm feeling joy again, stronger than ever before. I'm okay; I suppose as okay as I can be without you here, knowing you're there waiting for me. Having you there on the other side is a comfort and keeps me moving and looking up. Yet still, every once in a while, this heartache, this pain, will sneak up on me, grabbing and pulling me under. On those days, I crawl into bed and rest my tired soul.

No doubt you know I've made a fresh start and moved to Santa Monica to get away from the haunting of you and those trains. I'm glad I got out of Mountain View. A sad town full of big, rolling clouds and lost traces of you. It's your town, the place where I knew you. The town where you lived, the town where you died. A walking cemetery. In the months following your death, my nightly dreams of New York City hinted at my need to feel life around me, to return to the world of color, action, and the living. New York was out of the question—too cold, too stressful, too exhausting. I figured Los Angeles was the closest thing to New York on a beach. Every time I've been here, I've had fun. Since moving to California, I've had it in the back of my mind to start a private practice here one day. So why not go now? I moved in September, nine months after you passed and it's done me a world of good. The quality of sunlight is brighter than anywhere else I've lived. I'm writing my dissertation by the ocean, writing to you, and working at the Suicide Prevention Center on the hotline. I've learned the suicide assessment skills I wish I'd had with you. Now I know how to recognize your suicidal "invitations" and how I might have saved you. If that was even possible. I've gone over the weeks and months before your death so many times in my head. And I've saved you in hundreds of different ways. I've relived your death thousands of times.

But through my time trying to understand what happened, and through my work on the hotlines, and my research on suicide, I discovered the truth I wished I had seen earlier: you were practically programmed to self-destruct. You didn't know it. I didn't know it. You lived with so many risk factors for suicide. First off, you were sleep-deprived for months. You were physically abused as a child. You'd been dropped on your head at a young age. You suffered from childhood epilepsy. And at fifteen, you developed narcolepsy. Only after you died did I learn that 40 percent of people with narcolepsy kill themselves. Each one of these conditions, on its own, puts a person at risk for suicide. You had not just *one* of these risk factors but you had *all* of them. Put them together, and your suicide was inevitable. You also started taking the anti-depressant Prozac three days before your suicide. We now know definitively that anti-depressants can cause suicide ideation. Drug companies are even required to put a warning label on the bottle that these pills can potentially lead to suicide in young adults. Ultimately, even with all your risk factors, I think it was the anti-depressants that pushed you over the edge, almost like a body-snatch.

I can't begin to imagine the extent of the neurological confusion and disrepair in your brain. I can't fathom what it must've been like to be in your head, experiencing the world through so much static and with such a traumatized nervous system. Had I known then what I know now, you *know* I would have acted differently. Things might not have happened as they did. I would have prevented your death. I would've forced sleeping pills down your throat and guarded you and made sure you slept. I would've stopped you from taking anti-depressants. I would've paid for you to see a decent therapist (the one you saw was a moron). I would've paid for your acupuncture. I would've insisted you take your narcolepsy meds again.

I've beaten myself up for not knowing these risk factors then. I should've done my job better. And I forgive myself a little bit more each day for my ignorance, for my humanity. The truth is, I didn't know these things at the time. I was only human, not god, and not the world's most skilled psychologist. And I believe, on a spiritual level, that it was your destiny to kill yourself.

This past year, parts of myself I sort of knew were in me have grown and sprung into action, like discipline, faith, devotion, and strength. I'm becoming a woman I'm meant to be, the woman I've always been. By delving fully into my grieving I've finally made it through to the other side. And over here, I feel life more deeply, more passionately than ever before. I'm stronger. Focused. Driven. Determined. I will reach you one day. My life feels surreal. Entertaining. Fuzzy. Hilarious, even. The ride keeps going; it's only the view that changes. I enjoy my own company more than ever before. Most people haven't experienced this kind of shifting reality, and sometimes I find it hard to relate to the old way of things and to people who still live in my old world. Once you've lived through your own death, you can never go back. What stays constant is kindness, all forms of it budding everywhere; it never fails to stir movement from the cracks in my heart.

I've adjusted to the new terms and our new relationship, with you on the other side. Making meaning out of your death has been my lifeline. It's saved me. I've saved me. I kept making meaning and kept making meaning until my connection to the new world, the new story I told became stronger than the connection to my old way, my old story of the finality of death riddled with fear and pain. I simultaneously struggled to overcome my conditioning that sees physical death as the end of life, as terror unmasked. I don't believe in that anymore. While I grieved not being able to see you and touch you, I slowly began to allow and open to the reality where you are still very much alive, very much present with me wherever I go and in whatever I do. I feel you as my guardian angel. You know more about me than ever before. You hear my thoughts, you feel my feelings. We share the same heart. I have more faith in the invisible than ever before. Faith is the moment-to-moment commitment to the mystery. Feeling for you around me, I cultivate this commitment every day.

No matter what happens, I know I'll be okay. This is certain. If I can survive this, I can survive anything. I know who I am to the core. I know what I'm made of. I survived my existential nightmare. Here I am living without you, still breathing, heart still beating. I go on. I'm alive and continue to grow and expand and find new moments to appreciate. I continue to feel it all—the pain, the sorrow, the love, the mysterious beauty. It's like what you always wanted for me. To be so happy and fulfilled with myself that any man who came into my life would simply be the "icing on the cake." It took some time from when you first wished this for me. But here it is.

The other day I heard a line in a short film called *The Butterfly Circus* that pierced my heart-wound and made me cry:

The greater the struggle, the more glorious the triumph.

Love,
Sarah

....

Dear John,

From a spiritual perspective, suicide is a symptom of homesickness, an act of attempting to return home, to that oft-remembered nostalgic source. The one you never forgot. The place where I'll see you again.

Until then, I feel my home through beauty.

Love,
Sarah

....

Dear John,

I don't know if this is something you can help me with. People always say, "You need to let go," whatever that means. But *how* do I let go of you? I love you so damn much. I've loved you more than anyone in this world. Your suicide has caused me more pain and sorrow than I've ever known. How can I do that? How can I let you go?

Life is answering me in different ways—through emails, songs on the radio, updates on social media, and messages from you. The message I'm getting is that while I can let go of my past, the trauma of your suicide, and complete my grief, I can't actually fully let go of loving you. It's just not possible and there's no need. I'll always love you. You're a huge part of my life. And I'm accepting and allowing this to be so. Anything else would be a dishonoring of my experience with your death.

Love,
Sarah

John,

It's taken me a long time to come to this understanding and acceptance, but these days I'm a believer in fate, destiny, and "meant to be." Like, if it was meant to be, then it will be, and things have a way of working out for the best, even if it doesn't feel that way as things are unfolding. I know this can sometimes come across as harsh or overly simplistic, but the wise part of me truly believes this. I trust this; I know this. For whatever reason, you and I were not meant to be as romantic partners in this lifetime. Maybe some greater love is coming for me down the pipeline, I don't know. Maybe all will be uncovered in time. I don't know. Maybe it will all make perfect sense in hindsight, or all will be revealed when I cross over and have my big "after party." Who knows? And that doesn't mean that I can't still feel the tortured, angsty anguish of my unfulfilled love. I can argue with my fate endlessly, can't I? But I lose every time. You took your life and I am here carrying on. You're not coming back. I'm not coming to you. I accept this.

....

John,

I stand at the water's edge on this wide, empty beach in Santa Monica. Bluffs behind me, the waves roll in and out, never ceasing, never ending. I feel light, like I could fly. Seagulls soar past and you fly among them. A sense of peace fills me and quiets my mind. Your presence takes over and expands the contours and boundaries of my body, of my vision. Love overflows from my heart, tears stream down my face. My spirit grows. I fly with you, seeing the world through your eyes. This is my prayer and my guiding compass: to see the world as you see it now. All is golden and dazzling, everything perfectly as it should be.

Your suicide revealed the love you'd tirelessly reflected to us. The love I always saw in you, I now recognize in myself. As I walk without you, I carry your gift inside. You're a part of me now, in a way that wasn't possible before your death. I hope people can feel your light and kindness through me. It's now mine to share.

My heart is mending in spite of its damage, and my life goes on. The certainty of my death is inevitable. Until that day, I stand here, shoulders back, arms open, and offer you all the love in the world. You were the most beauty I've ever known. Thank you.

Your Tigerlily,
Sarah

the map:
guidance for beauty

At this stage in your grief you are most likely circling through acceptance of your beloved's death and going in and out of anger and depression. This roller coaster of anger, depression, and acceptance keeps going for a while. It's hard to say exactly how long this cyclical pattern will last. My roller coaster ride started easing up around the two-and-a-half-year mark. I still felt the loss and deeper, more nuanced layers of grief for another two and half years after that.

Maybe your grief lessens sooner and you find acceptance after a year or two. Maybe it takes you longer than five years. That's perfectly okay. Everyone grieves differently and at a different pace. The point of this stage is that you're finding some underlying peace with all that you've gone through, that life feels richer, and you have learned lessons through having endured tremendous pain and devastation. Ideally, you also have less fear around your own death and death in general, as you've had spiritual, transpersonal, and/or psychical experiences of connecting with your beloved on the other side, and you have faith in life after death. Hopefully, you have transcended or are in the process of transcending the societal and Western medical world conditioning that teaches us to fear death at all costs. If you can actively do this, it will bring you enormous comfort and relief.

MEDITATE

Hopefully you've begun some form of daily meditation sitting practice by now. If not, see the Transformational Practices and Resources section at the back of the book for some suggestions. Sitting regularly and receiving love from your beloved on the other side and from spirit is healing, expands your heart, and connects you to that other realm. You will also receive guidance about your path and your life through meditation. It's your bread and butter for healing.

SPEND TIME IN NATURE

I had my most transcendent moments at the beach, feeling connected with John's spirit or doing my own personal rituals of letting go on the beach (see more in the Transformational Practices section).

Spend time in nature, whichever kinds of nature soothe you the most. For me, it's beaches. For others it's mountains, woods, or desert. Sit quietly with nature and feel its essence fill you up. Find wonder in the small details and inhale the beauty into your body, mind, and spirit until you feel yourself expanding and almost becoming a part of the ocean or earth in front of you. Gazing at nature with your eyes relaxed for extended amounts of time can have a hypnotic and therapeutic effect on your brain state, making you feel lighter and more connected to the world around you. Fill yourself up with natural beauty.

CULTIVATE MAGIC

Let yourself feel wonder when you experience an unexplainable synchronicity or coincidence. Feel your heart in these moments and let the mystery light it up. Give yourself permission to feel love for the small things. Enjoy dusk and twilight hours, the "magic hours"—the liminal space, that in-between state between day and night that makes us feel like we're in between worlds and connects us to the mystery of life. When you are immersed in grief and missing someone you can't see, you are naturally in an in-between state of being. In between life and death. In between your old life and your new life. In between your old self and the new self you're becoming. Embrace the liminal space and commit to the not-knowing as if it is the only known. Allow faith to guide you through the mystery. Commit to the mystery. Make meaning out of the beauty of the natural world flitting by, the butterflies, fireflies, spiders, and rainbows. Let these moments reveal a story about your loved one in spirit. Talk to him. Dance with wonder at twilight on a tree-lined street as the warm afterglow of the sunset illuminates your path.

FEEL YOUR ALIVENESS

In our culture, we seem to be on a never-ending quest for happiness, yet depression rates continue to soar into the hundreds of millions. Growing up depressed, I was a seeker of happiness. I've come to discover that it's not happiness we seek, it's aliveness.

The antidote for depression isn't happiness, it's aliveness—feeling full, vibrant, and excited about life. Aliveness comes from the fusion of spirit and body. Our natural state of existence as humans. Let your spirit infuse your body and make it feel alive with sensations and beauty. Practice radical embodiment. Make sure you have some physical practices or outlets where you move your body and enjoy your senses. Music is beauty that can be absorbed easily by the body. Find the music that delights you, sparks you up, and makes you move.

BE IN CONNECTION

You may find that you feel most alive and connected to yourself and life when you're in connection with others. It's critical that you surround yourself with people whom you feel safe with and connected to. Feeling a sense of belonging—to yourself and others—is a crucial part of locating your place in the world and reason for being here, especially after a traumatic event.

This can be as simple as a daily phone call with a friend, seeing a trustworthy therapist who gets you, volunteering somewhere, babysitting, or sitting on a bench talking to stranger. Make sure that you have some form of authentic human connection every day that makes you feel like your life matters.

FOLLOW YOUR DREAMS, LITERALLY

Take note of any messages or images you see in your dreams. They may be clues as to which direction you may head in next. Three months after John died, I had a brief dream of a grey tabby cat curled up on my bed. When I woke up, I knew that that was my cat and I needed to find her. I searched cat shelters in the Bay Area until I connected with a little grey tabby named Hazel with whom I felt an instant connection. When I found her, I knew she was the one from the dream. She has large, innocent, seafoam-green eyes and she reminds me of John. She sits in meditation with me every day, she's social and loves people, and everyone who meets her is quite taken with her lovingness.

Even people who don't like cats. She's an angelic friend and protector, and I can't imagine having gone through this process without her by my side.

CONSIDER RELOCATING

After the initial trauma and intense grief has abated (usually around the first 6 months to a year), you may want to up and move and start over somewhere fresh—a place where you won't be weighed down by memories of your beloved. This did a world of good for me. It's always best to have a community set up before you move somewhere, however, be it a church, synagogue, meditation space, school program, or something else altogether. Ask friends and family to connect you with people in your new location.

CREATE YOUR PURPOSE

One of the most effective ways to make meaning out of your loss and pull yourself out of grief is to discover and create a sense of purpose that incorporates what you've learned from losing your beloved and sharing your wisdom with others. Having a clear sense of purpose is one of the most life-affirming measures you can take that will prevent suicidal thinking. People with a clear and motivated sense of purpose generally do not kill themselves (unless they are on prescription medication that makes them suicidal). Your purpose acts as a structure through which you can navigate time. Find a sense of purpose that feels authentic and also makes you feel good. That will allow you to transform your heartbreak into something valuable and spiritual that takes you beyond yourself. And this is the beauty.

....

Take your time in this *beauty* stage. There's no letting go of your love for your beloved; all you can do is feel your feelings fully, allow them to have their life, and then take baby steps forward.

SELF-LOVE IN THE AFTERMATH—2018

I'd been feeling rageful and mean-spirited of late for a variety of reasons. Anger had been in the air. I knew I had to get a Lomi Lomi massage—a traditional Hawaiian massage that's rhythmic and sensual, and that I just love. Most places on the mainland don't offer Lomi Lomi; when I googled it, I found just a couple of places that offered it, one of which was a spa in Santa Monica.

I called right away. "Hi, I'd like to book a Lomi Lomi massage for this afternoon," I said.

"Well we need to see if our masseuse is available," the receptionist said. "He's offsite. Let me call him."

She called back minutes later. He was available. We booked the massage for an hour later.

I waited on the massage table in my underwear and sheet for ten minutes past the appointed time. Finally, Robert rushed in, clunky and sweaty. He was a larger, darker-skinned man in a basic black shirt, baggy khaki pants, and white sneakers. He wore a slender gold band on his wrist with something written in Sanskrit. He had a huge, warm smile. He was a different-looking kind of masseuse; not your typical thin, healthy, LA-yogi-looking therapist. He got started right away.

I wondered where Robert drove in from, special for this appointment. I imagined him sitting in traffic for an hour, driving in from the other side of the city, then circling for parking and thus arriving the clichéd ten minutes late. Such is life in LA.

As the massage progressed, it became clear to me that this was anything but rhythmic and sensual. It was like Robert: clunky and sweaty. His white sneakers scraped against the wood floor as he earnestly ran around the table, working different limbs and oftentimes squatting in order to the get the angle just right. The squeaking of his sneakers made it hard for me to relax.

Eventually, I asked if he would mind taking off his shoes. He graciously agreed, adding that doing so would be better for him too.

Every now and again he checked in: "You doing okay?"

"Yes," I said each time.

But in my mind, I couldn't relax. I was angry, and kept chewing on the fact that this wasn't Lomi Lomi and wondering how much longer I would have to suffer through this sweaty, awkward massage. *Do I say something to the front desk?* I wondered. *Do I post something on Yelp about the service here? Do I do nothing?*

Patience, I told myself. *Find a way to just surrender and let it go. It will be over eventually, and none of this really matters. It's just a massage.*

As I lay there, half in my body, half in my mind, and as Richard kept enthusiastically working on me, I had this insight come to me: *If I truly love myself—like really, deeply, honestly love, adore, and honor myself, which has been my practice—then I would never intentionally harm myself. And so, by extension, if I love myself, then I could never kill myself.*

This sudden knowing of this truth in myself was a key that unlocked the darkness and dark thoughts hardwired into my DNA and genealogy laced with genetic and ancestral depression. It released me.

When Robert was finishing up, he placed three hot towels on me, using them to wipe off all the excess oil from the massage. He did everything with robust love and kindness.

When he was done, I got up from the table, got dressed, and met him downstairs in the lounge, where he'd set out tea and two apple slices for me.

I thanked him for his massage, and while paying the bill I proceeded to give him the usual 20 percent tip. I don't know if I'll ever see him again, but something about receiving touch from this truly kind and good-hearted man cracked me open. I felt compassion for his generosity and his humanness. It may not have been a Lomi Lomi, or even a good massage, but the way he gave the massage—the love and energy he put into it, and the effort he made to drive cross-town last minute—had turned out to be exactly what I needed.

I walked home quietly in the wind. I walked upstairs, lay down in bed, and cried—for all the pain and suffering I'd endured since I was a girl, for all the goodness and good intentions of my own heart, and for the suffering we all endure.

I've been free and clear of that anger and any lingering traces of suicidal thoughts ever since. My self-love wins the battle.

epilogue:

the path of the broken-hearted

There's a path only some of us seem to tread. It's not chosen but given, and requires more courage than most. As we move in the world, we are hit by loss in many forms—abandonment by a parent, the death of a child or a spouse before their time. Sorrow lives in us from an early age and we're not quite sure why. But we are innately more sensitive to heartbreak than others, feeling the loss of love as death.

The poet Rumi wrote that the cracks in our hearts are the places where light comes in. What if this is our entryway, our access point? Our way to know love. Our way to connect with the divine. How we grow. How we evolve. Then our job is to embrace the tears and know our sorrow as a form of love, rich with gifts and meaning, that can help us transform into the greatest version of ourself.

Not everyone walks this road or gets thrown on it. It's not for the faint of heart. It's sacred. For the bold, the courageous, the sensitive. Those who feel the most. The ones who have the ability to weave straw into gold and turn shit into poetry and magic. Let the heartbreak break you and kill you until you die. Your death makes you an alchemist. The reward is to know love on a level unknown to most and to appreciate the connections with loved ones in deeper ways. This is heartbreak's bittersweet gift—the gift you were willing to risk your life for.

Don't dismiss your burden or path lightly, for it's a sacred calling and will teach you of the beauty of the world. Trust it and feel the depths of your pain. Let it move you into the mystery of the unknown you yet to come. Take this time in the dark and honor its wisdom. You will emerge stronger, wiser, powerful. Healing your broken heart is the way toward the wholeness you crave.

Grieving is a completion of an incompleteness that can never be completed. This could take your whole life. The lessons are for you, specifically, and for your greatest embodiment.

....

This book is a tribute to an extraordinary and celestial man who lived his life in service of loving others but ultimately couldn't love himself. It is also an attempt to honor the spirit and innate beauty of all the dear loved ones we've loved and lost to suicide. Let's remember their unique humanity—their beauty and light, and also their darkness and flaws. They are neither one nor the other; rather, they encompass all aspects, death and love and every nuance of life in between. And through this simple fact of their humanity, they live on.

appendix a:
transformational practices

During my mourning, I had many practices that created a sacred container for my grief and helped shift my despair. This section provides more details about those practices. But before I go further, I'm putting out a disclaimer: some of the suggestions in this section are "spiritual" or more "woo-woo" than what you might find in other grief books. I encourage you to take what's useful to you and filter out what's not.

Creating some kind of healing "ritual" for yourself while going through deep grief is essential. By ritual, I mean doing something every day that has personal or spiritual meaning and shifts your emotions or energy for the better. Ideally, you should practice your daily rituals at the same time every day, be it in the morning or evening. The practices and consistency create an opportunity for release and transformation that is essential for guiding you through the dark. If you want to connect with your beloved in spirit on the other side, or your guides, it also establishes an appointment time, so to speak, where they know that you will be available and receptive to the energy and information coming through.

As I shared in some of the emails included in this book, my original intention with committing to a strong daily practice was to have an "awakening" so that time and my life would feel different and not feel like a burden until I could die and reunite with John. Initially, my spiritual practice was about reaching John and communicating with him on the other side. Now my spiritual practice is mostly about me—about connecting to myself, my soul, my guides and angels (of which John is one). My practice is about living more fully from my heart and experiencing joy and a deeper connection with life.

My list here is a suggested guideline. In my work as a psychologist, I offer my clients tools to create their own practices and then work with their unique gifts and proclivities to help them find what works for them. I hope you will explore some of these in your own way and time, and that you will also seek out the practices that feel right for you. The point is to be proactive and at the same time learn how to hold and embrace your pain and connect more fully within so that you can shift your grief.

PSYCHOTHERAPY AND TRAUMA WORK

This is crucial. You need a professional to hold space for your grief and to help you heal the trauma. They can be the same person or different therapists, depending on their expertise. The key to finding a good therapist is that you have to feel like he/she gets you and is a good fit. If you don't feel this way, therapy is not going to work.

SOMATIC EXPERIENCING, POINTS HOLDING PROCESS, AND EMDR

These are therapeutic modalities that specifically deal with trauma directly and efficiently. Somatic Experiencing and points holding involve direct touch from the therapist, and all three of these therapies release the trauma from where it's stored in the body: the nervous system. Until you release the trauma from your nervous system, you will continue to unconsciously attract people and events that recreate the same behavioral and emotional patterns related to the trauma—abandonment, loss, and codependency, to name a few.

Over the course of the nine months after John died and before I moved to Los Angeles, I worked with two different therapists. One was a transpersonally oriented therapist and utilized modalities such as authentic movement, art therapy, and gestalt work in addition to the usual talk therapy. I loved the authentic movement, as I'm partial to movement. And most of what was therapeutic about working with this therapist was that she held a lot of space for me to simply cry.

The second therapist was a Jungian expert specializing in symbols. I saw her on an occasional basis, and we mostly worked on understanding my dreams.

I looked for grief support groups, and sadly, there was a waiting list for the suicide survivors group. Ultimately, I decided to work directly with individual therapists instead. Grief groups can be helpful for some and challenging for others. If a group is all you have access to, then I recommend you go that route.

DAILY MEDITATION

After John's death, I began to practice meditation every morning for fifteen minutes and every night for fifteen minutes. I started by using a method called "The Presence Process," an eleven-week process for attaining more presence and for untangling the conditioning of the mind that goes back to early childhood. It was intense and challenged me to be very disciplined. It was not my favorite practice, but I do recommend it.

Over the years, my meditation techniques have changed, but I still sit and meditate diligently every morning.

SHAMANIC WORK + RITUAL

While I was working through my grief, I started working with a shaman in San Francisco named Liv Wheeler. She was trained in the Burkina Faso tradition by renowned shaman Malidoma Somé. Liv often channeled John and communicated with my ancestors and other beings on the other side, and together, we were able to make some sense out of what had happened. She was instrumental in helping me learn and grow through my grief. She helped me open a doorway into a magical way of being in the world that is not airy-fairy or a "delusional" side effect of grieving but rather rooted and grounded in an ancient, shamanistic cultural heritage practice that's deeply connected to nature and interconnected with the realm of Spirit. I learned these new ways from Liv, and they inspired me to cultivate a new relationship with the invisible—one that is manifested through objects, nature, and ritual.

Liv facilitated a variety of healing processes on me, including soul retrieval: scouting out lost parts of my soul that had broken off over the years as a result of trauma or fear. She said she found a lost soul piece that had left when I was twenty-nine, right after John passed. Liv also found and reintegrated other parts of me that had left at earlier ages. Whether you believe in this or not, all I can say is that I felt lighter, more intact, and once again inspired by the possibilities of the infinite and miracles after doing this work.

Liv often had me do "homework," usually in the form of some sort of ritual she wanted me to practice. For instance, she told me to take wine, chocolate, and flowers to the beach and sit and have a picnic with John and make offerings of flowers and a picture of him to the ocean. Another assignment was to gather with my friends and ask each of them to tell me how they saw me. That was hard, terrifying, and embarrassing, but ultimately helped me feel acknowledged and seen as I was emerging through the dark. Being seen and acknowledged for what we are experiencing is very important. I cannot emphasize this enough.

Liv taught me several practices and rituals to do every morning during my daily morning practice. She taught me how to make offerings to my guides and angels, the elements of spirit, and John. I bought a small black garden bench and with it created an altar in my living room where I placed photos of John and any special objects—crystals, feathers, poems, flowers, or books—that were meaningful to me. Each morning before I meditated, I placed a bowl on the altar and poured offerings into it.

There are many teachings about different offerings; they vary from culture to culture and shamanic lineage. I'm not familiar with all these teachings, but I based my choices on my work with Liv, loosely copying what I'd seen her do. She usually made offerings of ash that had been created during a special ritual. I had no access to this kind of ash, so the ash was out. She also made offerings of some kind of alcohol to her ancestors. I knew that John loved red wine and my grandfather loved scotch, so I alternated between these two. Liv told me that I have a posse of angels that surround me and that I'm most guided by the angelic realm. She also said that angels like sweets, so I also made offerings of honey or sugar. Cinnamon was one of John's favorite foods—he used to put it on everything—so I also offered cinnamon.

The process looked like this: I welcomed (out loud or in my head) John, spirit, my guides, my ancestors, my angels, the earth spirits, water spirits, air spirits, and fire spirits into the space. One by one, step by step, I announced that I was making an offering of wine and then took a sip, spit it into the bowl, and then poured some into the bowl. Then I would pour the honey into the bowl, and next the cinnamon and whatever else it might be—flowers or something else Liv had suggested. I ended with an offering of water.

After making the invocation and giving the offerings, I sat quietly, eyes closed, and noticed any sensations around me in the air. Did the temperature change? Did I feel something move? Did I feel an itch? Did it feel like I had a hair fall on my face? This one I felt a lot, like a hair falling over my lip, and when I'd touch my mouth to move it, there was nothing there. I would get chills or goose bumps *a lot.* This is pretty common with mediums or people who are in touch with loved ones on the other side. I paid attention to images that came to me in my mind's eye.

With my eyes closed, I often feel and see light, lots and lots of light. John was very light and bright when he was in a body, and when I feel and see a tingling, warm, bright light, I know it's John. And he comes a lot. Much of the time during my sitting practice, I sit and feel goose bumps all over my body and see and feel a warm light and feel flooded with a sense of love. It feels amazing. But it can also be hard to feel so much love, especially when there's so much grief associated with it. It can bring up a lot of emotion. Oftentimes when I bask in John's love, I am overwhelmed by tears (of all kinds) and sit and cry and cry. It can be hard, but it's also healing and feels good. I just go with it.

I think sitting and basking in the love, goose bumps, tears, and light pouring through us from our loved one on the other side (or from whatever source) is the most healing and essential part of any sitting practice—for everyone, not just those who have lost someone and are grieving.

CULTIVATING PSYCHIC ABILITIES, SIGNS, AND SYNCHRONICITIES

After I made my offerings, I expressed thanks for things in my life that I appreciated and thanked everyone for all of their help. I got as specific as I could. Then I'd ask for help with certain things that I was working on or struggling with. A big one that I asked for was help in cultivating my psychic abilities and help knowing, really knowing beyond a shadow of a doubt, that John was still alive. This was hugely important to me. I asked for signs from him to show me that he was still alive. I asked for ways in which I could grow to be able to see him, feel him, and hear him as strongly as possible. I asked for help in eliminating my intellectual, skeptical, and doubting mind-filter. I asked for strength, guidance, clarity, and other qualities for my healing. I usually asked to be able to see John again or asked to have a dream about him. Sometimes, I talked about a dream I'd had and then asked for guidance in understanding the messages of the dream. Then I'd sit and allow myself to receive an answer or imagine the answer as best as I could.

Other times, I practiced imagery/visualization exercises, like imagining a gold ball in my mind's eye and holding it there for as long as possible. This was to help sharpen my inner-seeing, clairvoyant sense. I also practiced listening and hearing all the sounds around me—as many as possible, and from as far away as possible. I played with how I could magnify these sounds. How could I hear things that were even farther away? This was to develop my clairaudient abilities (or inner hearing senses) so that I could communicate with John and hear what he was saying to me. I also practiced this by simply listening to whatever thoughts came into my head.

For many months, I struggled with doubts about what I was hearing and receiving. I thought that I was probably making things up, and that the things that I was hearing were obviously not John. And even if it was John, I was missing a lot of what he was saying; I felt I could only make out a few things here and there, and the things I was hearing were only what I wanted to hear. I wrestled with my innate and New York-conditioned skepticism and doubt—especially my self-doubt. My mental filter was still too strong.

Because of this, on top of all the grief and pain I was experiencing, I beat myself up by calling myself "crazy" for "hearing" and communicating with John. Surely I was insane and none of this was real. I couldn't trust my intuitive or clairaudient abilities, even though I'd had so many varying experiences over the years and so much proof with my own eyes. I kept asking for more "bizarre" contact and proof that John was still alive in some form because my mental, rational, old way of being—my conditioning and the criticism I'd received and internalized over the years—had such a strong hold that I couldn't let myself believe or allow myself to have faith.

I kept asking John for signs of his presence, and they came: electricity blew out in my kitchen; candles exploded; and a variety of other weird things, almost too unbelievable to write about here, took place too. But I also worked on this process in therapy. My therapist helped me understand the origins of my need for "proof" and analysis and making sure that everything was rational and sane. I learned and acknowledged what purpose that role had served in my life—how it was a formerly necessary adaption that, given my current situation, was no longer relevant.

I worked on my doubt with Liv, too. She assured me that my abilities and experiences were real and in fact were coming from John, time and time again. She and I practiced my communication with him together, and she confirmed that what I was hearing was in fact what was being said. She was the one who pointed out that the only thing blocking me was my mind, which was acting as a "filter" and blocking the flow of messages from John and spirit. I was negating what I was receiving before I even let it have a chance to come through. I just had to *trust* a little, let it be, and see what happened. When I did, I would often hear songs in the air right before they came on the radio or words that were about to be spoken.

So for me, practicing this ability was not so much about practicing "making things up" or guessing, but more about practicing getting out of my own way and allowing what was already there to move through me without stonewalling it. It was a deeper practice of allowing, trusting, and believing (especially in myself), which of course healed and continues to heal all aspects of my life and facilitates exponential growth spurts.

And so every morning, I asked for guidance around letting go of my mental filter and for help releasing doubts, skepticism, and cynicism so that I could open to and receive and flow with whatever communication and guidance I was getting. This growing faculty is another odd gift of John's death, and one I still work on actively.

I also read a bunch of books about channeling and being a medium and shamanism. These were helpful because they gave me practical techniques and anecdotal evidence for my questioning mind, and also because they provided context and "theory" for what I was studying. The more I read, the more it opened up my imagination, and that was crucial in developing these abilities, because John would sometimes share things that he is/was doing over there on the other side that I had no reference point for or way of imagining from my limited perspective. I had to keep taking my imagination to places it had never been before.

FORGIVENESS MEDITATION

Forgiving yourself for your humanity of not having been able to save your loved one is an important step in the first years of your healing. Forgiving your loved one for taking their life is also important and may take time.

For this meditation, you may want to make a voice memo of yourself reading this slowly so you can then listen with headphones, covering your eyes, and get the most benefits from it.

....

Take a deep breath. Notice, in this moment, any tension that's showing up in your body. Check in with your body. Feel your feet on the ground. Feel your body pressed against the chair you're sitting in. The process of forgiveness is a process of the heart.

I want to invite you to breathe into the heart as often as you can remember.

Get comfortable. Close your eyes. Breathe into your body, into your heart.

As you breathe into your heart, feel your heart expanding with every breath. Growing with every breath. Expanding until it expands large enough that your body can fit inside your heart. Breathe into your heart until it feels large enough that you could fit the whole room inside your heart.

{pause}

Look there. All of a sudden, your heart is the most lusciously decked out room you've ever seen. All red velvet, with soft couches and pillows and satin. Just the softest, most luxurious place you've ever seen.

When you get that image, I want you to call yourself by name, in your own inner room, in your own mind. Call yourself by name and invite yourself to come in and take ease in your heart. See yourself entering into that soft space and just reclining. Resting.

{pause}

Calling yourself by name, say, "I forgive you. I forgive you for everything you've ever done, intentionally or unintentionally, that caused pain. I forgive you for everything you've ever said. Yes even that, that has caused pain."

{pause}

Call yourself by name again. Say, "I forgive you even for the things you have thought that have been less than flattering and beautiful about others or yourself. I forgive you. I take you into my heart just as you are. I accept you, just as you are. Here and now."

{pause}

When you have a sense that you've taken this in, that you're reclining in your own heart—resting at last—see yourself gently and easily rise up off the pillows. Envision a golden road, like the setting sun on the ocean. See yourself walking down that golden road. And as you walk, bless yourself: May you be happy. May you be free from suffering. May you be at peace.

Breathing into the heart. Feeling your own heart-space. Your own red velvet room. Acknowledge for yourself the act of power that you've just engaged in. What you've just done is released yourself from the bondage of anger and resentment that you've carried toward yourself. And you can even say it to yourself: "I release this resentment. I let go of everything I no longer need."

Breathe *again*. Feel your body, feel the ground—this physical space. And open your eyes and come back into the room.

DREAM JOURNAL + OTHER JOURNALS

During the first six months after John passed, I had a very active dream life—lots of dreams about John, and many dreams about New York City. I kept a dream journal and recorded my dreams every day. I could tell that something major was happening in my dream life and in my unconscious, and I wanted to learn the language that my dreams were speaking in and work with a trusty translator. It was very much like learning a new language.

In addition to keeping a dream journal, I kept two other journals. One was for the regular journaling I did every night, and the other was to log the signs and synchronicities and messages I was receiving from John on the other side. I felt I had to write them down so I didn't lose or forget them, especially for the years to come.

Writing has been enormously therapeutic for me, and the writing of this book has also helped me understand my pain, hold my pain, and connect the dots around John's suicide. It has helped me keep him alive as well—which, during the grieving process, provided me with comfort and buffered the totality of my loss. Some may want to say that this could delay acceptance of John's death. However, arriving at acceptance takes time and cannot be preemptively forced. Keeping John's memory alive for a while honored me and his life. It was part of my healing and actually gave me the time and space needed to process his death and understand who he was more fully. I simply could not let go until I was ready.

ACUPUNCTURE + BODYWORK

In the first few months, I went to acupuncture because my energy was very low. This was helpful. Working with a bodyworker— massage therapist, chiropractor, Reiki master, or any other kind of therapeutic practitioner—is another helpful layer of support and self-care. The body is going through its own grief, especially if it is adjusting to a sudden lack of physical intimacy it is accustomed to, and it needs to be touched and supported therapeutically.

SPIRITUAL GUIDANCE

I saw a spiritual guide on a few occasions, but eventually he wasn't helpful because it was obvious he didn't get what my pain or grief was like. Spiritual guidance can be helpful if you have a spiritual guide or teacher with whom you connect—someone whose wisdom resonates with you. Meditation teachers, shamans, facilitators, clergy, rabbi, etc. can guide you through the grieving process, but only if trust and rapport is established and he/she feels like the right fit for you and understands your loss.

SACRED PLANT-MEDICINE WORK

My move to Los Angeles put me in contact with an LA-based shaman from Peru. He facilitates ceremony groups by working with a wide variety of sacred plants, such as ayahuasca, psilocybin, and San Pedro. Each plant has a divine intelligence capable of penetrating any core wounding or breaks in the spiritual, emotional, energetic, and soul bodies and brings the patterns of dysfunction and trauma up to awareness for integration. These ceremonies and the uses of sacred plants as ritual and spiritual practice are about experiencing a sense of home within oneself.

Through my work with the plants and this shaman, and after being embraced by a deep, loving, and gifted community of other spiritual seekers and practitioners, I have been able to open my heart again to men. I've learned how to feel safe within myself; how to trust the world again; how to feel safe with men; and how to feel safe in relationships. I'm learning how to be loved. The plants and the community have reflected to me my own inner and outer beauty. And within this sense of love and beauty, I've claimed an aliveness that I've never felt before. It's the opposite of depression and suicidality. It's a feeling of exuberance—the wild ecstasy of feeling my feet in the sand, of dancing up and down as I gaze at the night sky listening to music through my headphones. The plant-work has facilitated my own knowing of the gift of aliveness.

According to the shaman I worked with, approximately 120,000 sacred ceremonies happen around the U.S. in a given month. It's a very specific kind of calling and healing practice, and if you feel called to do this work, I recommend doing some research and finding a shaman whose values, perspectives, and teachings have integrity and feel in alignment with you. Also make sure that you have a community to support your process, because the plants will often show you your own inner hells before they take you to other more uplifting states like bliss.

Transformation through plant-work is evolutionary: it shifts the frequency of our consciousness and shows us new ways of being—more loving, open-hearted versions of ourselves. As humans, our ways of treating each other have not changed much since the Middle Ages. We still feel threatened by the minor annoyances and disagreements about each other's personal beliefs and viewpoints. We still murder; we still lie, cheat, and attack one another physically, emotionally, and verbally. Our behavior has not evolved. The time has come for us to make more conscious choices by clearing out all the old pain and wounding that blocks us and keeps us in repetitive patterns of dysfunction. Working with plants reveals what is unconscious in us faster than any therapeutic modality, and therefore we can release that stale, heavy energy and emotional pain, heal the wounds fully, and be less hindered by old, negative, habitual behaviors. And thus, we can actually start to evolve.

Some people get addicted to this kind of work, so it's important to note that work with plants should be done judiciously. When you feel you've reached a certain level of healing and completeness, you should take a break and integrate the lessons. This need not be an endless path.

DANCE

I dance at least once, often two times a week at classes called 5 Rhythms, Soul Motion, or Ecstatic Dance. Each week, in cities and towns all over the world (if you look it up, you can find one by you), a specially trained DJ plays sets of amazing, diverse songs from all genres—hip-hop, trance, pop, soul, rock, world, and more—and facilitates a movement practice. In a 5 Rhythms class, songs are played in sets that correspond to five different rhythms: Flow, Staccato, Chaos, Lyrical, and Stillness. It's embodied meditation meets wild dance party. It lasts two to three hours. There's no alcohol available or sold on the premises. People let it rip. Some skip around like little kids; others just wiggle a finger in the air; holler and scream; and then there are those that appear to be on something but aren't, caressing each other's face while lying on the floor. It's an anything goes type of thing; you can dance solo, couple up, or sit in the middle and just watch.

COMMUNITY + BELONGING

Being a part of a community that mirrors who you are—your values, your spirituality, and your general ways of being—is hugely important for your healing. I never felt a sense of belonging to the community I was raised in (modern orthodox Jewish); I have felt isolated and alienated for most of my life, and consequently struggled with depression and existential loneliness. After John died, my community at grad school disappeared. People went their separate ways as they moved on with their lives. I felt mostly alone and isolated in my grief, and I spent most of my time huddled in my apartment.

After moving, it took me some time to find a community of like-minded spiritual practitioners and seekers in Los Angeles. But once I did, my life changed drastically for the better. The simple fact of being part of a community and feeling embraced and seen by them, especially in my grief and through my deeper shadowy layers, helped me feel more integrated and whole—less alone in the world.

I cannot overemphasize the importance of being in community and feeling a sense of belonging. This could be the single most important piece of your healing—to be surrounded by loving, caring people and to feel like you matter; to know that your feeling of belonging won't go away, no matter what you do.

If you feel isolated or disconnected from people and community, I urge you to find a community somewhere, whether it be through a grief support group, a community center, a yoga center, a church, a school, or your work. The community must feel familiar and safe, and you should feel embraced by the people you are with. Isolation is a huge problem in our society, and is a huge contributor to the depression so many people suffer from. Grief is an inherently lonely, dislocating, and isolating experience. The remedy for this is to grieve in community.

....

Over the years, my practices have shifted and changed as I've changed. I like to keep things fluid and adaptable, not rigid or dogmatic. I've let go of the ritual of offering wine, water, and so on to the ancestors and element spirits. But I do still intentionally connect with spirit every morning and offer gratitude for the help, guidance, wisdom, and inspiration it brings to my life. I pray, too, in the sense that I talk about what's going on and I ask questions and wait for answers. I set my intentions for the day and ask for help with specific things.

My dance continues to transform and empower me, and I go in and out of therapy. I completed seven years of training with a Peruvian shaman, and I find new teachings and teachers every year. I hope that your experience surviving suicide initiates your spiritual journey or deepens it; I hope that you cultivate your own unique healing practices and, in doing so, find your way through the dark.

appendix b:
resources

BOOKS ON MEDITATION

A New Earth—Eckhart Tolle
The Power of Now—Eckhart Tolle
Loving What Is—Byron Katie
The Presence Process: A Journey into Present Moment Awareness—
   Michael Brown
The Untethered Soul: The Journey Beyond Yourself—
   Michael A. Singer
The Surrender Experiment: My Journey Into Life's Perfection—
   Michael A. Singer
Full Catastrophe Living—Jon Kabat-Zinn
Dipa Ma: The Life and Legacy of a Buddhist Master—
   Amy Schmidt
Letting Go: The Pathway of Surrender—David R. Hawkins

BOOKS ON LIFE AFTER DEATH

Dying to Be Me: My Journey From Cancer, to Near Death, to
   True Healing—Anita Moorjani
All books by George Anderson

FORGIVENESS

Forgive for Good—Dr. Fred Luskin
Forgive for Love—Dr. Fred Luskin

RECOMMENDED MEDIUMS

George Anderson
www.georgeanderson.com

Rebecca Rosen
www.rebeccarosen.com

Felix Lee Lerma
www.felixleelerma.com

HEALING AND MANIFESTATION

www.tobemagnetic.com

acknowledgements

I'd like to thank my family, friends, therapists, and healing practitioners who helped support me in various different ways in the aftermath of John's death: Elana, Deena, Peter, Naomi, Kat, Pam, Shoshana, Daniela, Rob, Mailan, Neeti, Wes, Mike, Liv, Fred L., Christine E., Michele R., Patricia S., Henry L.. Watching a loved one survive a devastating suicide is not an ordinary occurrence, and knowing how to be supportive, I imagine, is scary and confusing. Thank you for staying with me. Without your connection and support, I'm not sure how things would've fared.

Countless people over the years provided sessions or held space for my grief and healing, and I'm grateful for all of it. Sending a big thank you to the village at large.

Thank you to my team at Spark Press—Brooke Warner and Samantha Strom for making the publication process seamless. And thank you to my editor Krissa Lago for all your guidance and input.

about
the author

Dr. Sarah Neustadter is a psychologist based in Venice Beach, Los Angeles, who specializes in spiritual development, suicide survivor grief, unblocking creativity, and millennial issues. Her website is www.sarahneustadter.com.

Author photo © Chris Loomis

about
sparkpress

SparkPress is an independent, hybrid imprint focused on merging the best of the traditional publishing model with new and innovative strategies. We deliver high-quality, entertaining, and engaging content that enhances readers' lives. We are proud to bring to market a list of *New York Times* best-selling, award-winning, and debut authors who represent a wide array of genres, as well as our established, industry-wide reputation for creative, results-driven success in working with authors. SparkPress, a BookSparks imprint, is a division of SparkPoint Studio LLC.

Learn more at GoSparkPress.com

SELECTED TITLES FROM SPARKPRESS

SparkPress is an independent boutique publisher delivering high-quality, entertaining, and engaging content that enhances readers' lives, with a special focus on female-driven work. www.gosparkpress.com

Mission Afghanistan: An Army Doctor's Memoir, Elie Cohen, translation by Jessica Levine. $16.95, 978-1-943006-65-6. Decades after evading conscription as a young man, Franco-British doctor Elie Paul Cohen is offered a deal by the French Army: he can settle his accounts by becoming a military doctor and serving at Camp Bastion in Afghanistan.

The House that Made Me: Writers Reflect on the Places and People That Defined Them, edited by Grant Jarrett. $17, 978-1-940716-31-2. In this candid, evocative collection of essays, a diverse group of acclaimed authors reflect on the diverse homes, neighborhoods, and experiences that helped shape them—using Google Earth software to revisit the location in the process.

Gravel on the Side of The Road: True Stories From a Broad Who Has Been There, Kris Radish. $15, 978-1-940716-43-5. A woman who worries about carrying a .38 special in her purse, nearly drowns in a desert canyon, flies into the war in Bosnia, dances with the FBI, and spends time with murderers, has more than a few stories to tell. This daring and revealing adventured by beloved novelist Kris Radish is her first book of autobiographical essays.

Quiet the Rage: How Learning to Manage Conflict Will Change Your Life (and the World), Richard Burke. $22.95, 978-1-943006-41-0. Where there are people, there is conflict—but conflict divides people. Here, expert Certified Professional Coach R.W. Burke helps readers understand how conflict works, how they themselves may actually be the source of the conflict they're experiencing in their lives, and, most important, how to stop being that source.

A Story That Matters: A Gratifying Approach to Writing About Your Life, Gina Carroll. $16.95, 9-781-943006-12-0. With each chapter focusing on stories from the seminal periods of a lifetime—motherhood, childhood, relationships, work, and spirit—*A Story That Matters* provides the tools and motivation to craft and complete the stories of your life.